# In the Morning, WHEN I RISE

## From Loss to Anointing

R. G. Shelton

WestBow
PRESS

*WestBow Press books may be ordered through booksellers or by contacting:*

*WestBow Press*
*A Division of Thomas Nelson*
*1663 Liberty Drive*
*Bloomington, IN 47403*
*www.westbowpress.com*
*1-(866) 928-1240*

*Because of the dynamic nature of the Internet, any Web addresses or links contained in this book may have changed since publication and may no longer be valid. The views expressed in this work are solely those of the author and do not necessarily reflect the views of the publisher, and the publisher hereby disclaims any responsibility for them.*

*ISBN: 978-1-4497-0078-2 (sc)*
*ISBN: 978-1-4497-0080-5 (hc)*
*ISBN: 978-1-4497-0079-9 (e)*

*Library of Congress Control Number: 2010926334*

*Printed in the United States of America*

*WestBow Press rev. date: 2/1/2013*

# Dedication

I would first like to thank and dedicate this book to the Most High God, who gave me the words, direction, strength, and power to endure and to write this book.

To my husband who fought the battle with me: I love you dearly.

To my beautiful blessings, "my double for my trouble," Zoe and Simone: thank you for filling our lives with so much joy, laughter, and restoration. God is so amazing.

To my parents, who trained me up the way that I should go and allowed me to watch them transform into what God has called them to be.

To my grandparents and all of those who came before and walked in accordance with the will of God, allowing the anointing of their covenant to cover me: I say, "Thank you." You all knew, as I now know, that God is the greatest treasure we have on this earthly journey.

To all of my siblings, in-laws, family and friends who I love so much and am so grateful to have – I love you all.

Last but by no means least, I want to thank my angel Madison, the greatest of my beloveds, the most beautiful, loving, and strong spirit I have ever come to love: Thank you. I am because *you are*. I love you with all of my being and appreciate your blessedness.

Ms. Madison Shelton
April 29, 2006–June 12, 2007

# Our Biggest Fear

"Our biggest fear is not that we are inadequate. Our biggest fear is that we are powerful beyond measure. It is our light, not our darkness, that most frightens us. We ask ourselves, who am I to be brilliant, gorgeous, talented and fabulous? "You are a Child of God. Your playing small does not serve the world. There's nothing enlightened about shrinking so that other people won't be insecure around you. We were born to make magnificent the glory of God that is within us. It's not just in some of us, it is in everyone. And as we let our own light shine, we unconsciously give others permission to do the same. As we are liberated from our own fears, our presence automatically liberates others."

Marianne Williamson

# Introduction

*And He said, Go out and stand on the mount before the Lord. And behold, the Lord passed by, and a great and strong wind rent the mountains and broke in pieces the rocks before the Lord, but the Lord was not in the wind; and after the wind an earthquake, but the Lord was not in the earthquake; and after the earthquake a fire, but the Lord was not in the fire; and after the fire [a sound of gentle stillness and] a still, small voice. When Elijah heard the voice, he wrapped his face in his mantle and went out and stood in the entrance of the cave. And behold, there came a voice to him and said, What are you doing here, Elijah?* (1 Kings 19:11)

Losing my 13-month old daughter to cancer was the worst thing that has ever happened to me. While going through my most challenging personal storm, I was bound into relationship with God like I never could have imagined.

The weight of my loss pressed me down so far that I did not know if I would make it at the end. I stayed in prayer and meditation constantly and in turn, I was brought into the awareness of His spirit, His voice. There was such a yawning void inside me. What else was there but to offer that void up to God Who filled me with visions, dreams and His precious Holy Spirit?

When we are going through a storm, suddenly we find ourselves holding on to the Lord with everything we have inside. Now, we realize He is our only hope and we go to our Father in our time of need truly seeking Him and His direction, and it is at that moment that our greatest resurrection happens.

It happens because we are in a place where brokenness has occurred and we are now willing vessels to be bent and reshaped. During that desperate hour, we spend our time soaking up His Word full of His knowledge and truth, encouraging ourselves and filling ourselves with His Spirit. Often in peaceful times, we get caught up in everyday cycles and the flame of our love for God is not as intense as it could be. Earthly things overwhelm us and take up our time, causing us to almost forget who we are and from where we have come.

Writing this book caused me to relive the pain of losing Madison all over again. Knowing I was okay and that the storm was over did not comfort me. The torment of those days assaulted me afresh. I needed time for what I knew in my soul to be accepted by my heart – my spirit.

A year after healing and restoration began, I picked up this book and went back to work on it.

I was again walking in faith and was further along in the healing process, but I was now walking in peace. The flame was not as hot as it could have been, but my faith was on the rise. What I needed was consistency and more passion in Bible study and devotional time.

As I began reading through the many notebooks and journals I'd written during and since that storm, God's Word—with which I'd filled myself day-in and day-out in hospital rooms and in the quiet stillness of my home—began its transforming work. There was a re-igniting of my passion to do this book, not just for myself, but for others. And, I realized that in doing for others so that someone else could be free and walk in their anointing, I was also blessing myself.

Going through those journals, the hunger for knowledge - the hunger for the wisdom of God - that answers the questions of this life stirred in me.

This story would be a blessing to me and not only encourage me, but cause me to bless others in return. What I do for others, God does for me. When I present the truth of God's Word to others, I discover His truth for myself. I am inviting you to make this journey with me, because whatever your personal challenges are, we are traveling the same road, heading toward the same destination: peace and life through Jesus Christ our Lord and Savior.

Whether your storm is composed of thunder and lightning or is of earthquake magnitude, you're waiting for that quiet whisper. In that quiet whisper, God met me where I was, restored me, blessed me and caused everything to work out for my good. He's doing that for you too.

Be encouraged. Take heart in the fact that tomorrow will be better. Know for a fact that faith works, no matter what your eyes see right now. Know that when God whispers in your spirit, hold on to His Word. His will for you is wonderful. He has everything you need. There's more joy in Him than in the life we try to create without Him. God is love and we are so important to Him that He has even numbered the hairs on our heads!

He lives in us and the quiet whisper we hear in our spirit is Him leading us to our destiny. He speaks nothing but life to us and keeps His promises to us through His Word.

When Elijah was on the mountain, the Lord told him:

*Go out, and stand before me on the mountain. And as Elijah stood there, the Lord passed by, and a mighty windstorm hit the mountain. It was such a terrible blast that the rocks were torn loose, but the Lord was not in the wind. After the wind there was an earthquake, but the Lord was not in the earthquake. And after the earthquake there was a fire, but the Lord was not in the fire. And after the fire there was the sound of a gentle whisper. When Elijah heard it, he wrapped his face in his cloak and went out and stood at the entrance of the cave. And a voice said, What are you doing here, Elijah?* (1 Kings 19:11–13).

The storm, the earthquake, or the fire…God was not in them. Stand still with Elijah. Stand still, holding on to faith and listen for the gentle whisper. God has led you to this place – don't move, wait for Him. God will sustain you, deliver you and bless you.

Come, let's walk together through my journey and your journey, and may we strengthen one another and stand strong. Hear the voice of the Lord and know that you are here for a purpose. May we be blessed on this journey— together.

## Chapter 1

# Under the Juniper Tree

*Teach me, O LORD, the way of Your statutes, and I shall keep
it to the end. Give me understanding, and I shall keep Your law;
indeed, I shall observe it with my whole heart. Make me walk in
the path of Your commandments, for I delight in it. Incline my
heart to Your testimonies, and not to covetousness. Turn away my
eyes from looking at worthless things, and revive me in Your way.
Establish Your word to Your servant, who is devoted to fearing
You. Turn away my reproach which I dread, for Your judgments
are good. Behold, I long for Your precepts; revive me in Your
righteousness (Psalm 119:33–40).*

FOR YEARS, I HEARD GOD calling me into a relationship
with Him. I knew the life I was living was not what God
wanted for me. I knew God had better things for me. But it
was a carefree life and I did what I wanted, how I wanted.
I did not want to be held accountable for my choices and
actions. I thought that I would not have any fun and would
not be so full of life if I lived according to His plan. Like
many, I would get with God later - you know - when I was
old and could not do anything else. I had allowed myself to
believe that I could not be satisfied with just God.

I mean, I went to church, *said* I believed in Him, and
did all the things that religious folks do. But I just would not
wade in that "deep water." I did not check out the Bible for
myself to confirm or deny what I thought. So, I stayed pretty

1

superficial in my dealings with the Lord. I knew I could not run forever, but I would run as long as I could.

To tell the truth, we run because we are scared to death to get into relationship with God. Sure, He forgives our sins, but does God really forget them? Do we? Do others? And the thought of completely giving God our lives to do with as He pleases...well, that's a lot to chew on.

My running slowed to a jog and things began to change. My running buddies and hangouts started to disturb my spirit. The things I did, my views about life and people, and what I believed began to make me uneasy.

I had been operating in what the Bible calls "the flesh" – the part of us that's more concerned about the here and now than with spiritual things. Suddenly, the friends I thought were funny now seemed vulgar; their jokes were coarse and not funny. The clever and strong-minded were just plain sneaky, liars, and weak-minded, wearing thin masks. Not only was I myself changing, but changing relationships, lifestyles, jobs, addresses – everything! Change, change, change! Work, work, work!

I have to tell you, I fought God on this and did what was easiest for me for a long while: I lied to myself. I said everyone is the same - my friends are like everyone else. *Even if I change*, I told myself, *everyone else will still be doing what they are doing, so why change friends only to get others like them?* I don't do what they do, say everything they say, go everywhere they go, and that should be good enough. If I stop hanging with them, isn't that being judgmental? I am not better than they are, am I? These stupid ideas were a trick of the enemy.

I realized that it is not judging people I was confronted with, but judging sin. They were fast becoming unequally yoked relationships. I needed to deal with the truth. Because of the Lord, I was making better, more conscientious kinds of decisions. If I continued to live life contrary to God, I would eventually go back to the way I'd been living. My one spoon of sugar would not sweeten the bitter tea. I had to stop lying to myself.

For someone who did not care about what people said, what folks said was more important than I cared to admit. Why else would I not change? I was living in self-delusion. This mentality was also fostered by radio and television talk shows, music, and self-proclaimed gurus, pedaling the earthly life: comfort in our sin. That is insanity which leads to spiritual death. The enemy is a great salesman.

When I look at my life, I recognize the constant conflict in my spirit; that toil that is a part of our daily existence and progression. What I went through was a spiritual battle – a battle for the mind. We are always in pursuit of God's mind. That is the one we want:

*"For My thoughts are not your thoughts, Nor are your ways My ways," says the LORD." For as the heavens are higher than the earth, So are My ways higher than your ways, And My thoughts than your thoughts* (Isaiah 55:8-9).

However, there is an enemy to this acquisition. When we speak of the "enemy" we are not talking about a comical little red demon. The devil is not a cartoon, there are no characters with red bodies and long tails or pitchforks that sit on your shoulder or hide behind doors, nor are there tall skinny guys in black cloaks and long white faces. I am talking about a spirit.

We ourselves are spirit (Genesis 2:7), and there is a constant battle between spirit and flesh and soul (mind). There is a struggle between God and the spirit of man (Genesis 6:3). There is a battle between our old nature and our new nature in Christ (Colossians 3:5). Each day that we win the battle, we move to a more intense level of peace and completeness. What usually makes this battle more difficult is that most of us cannot recognize it for what it is – spiritual warfare. If we do not understand that the battle is spiritual and the weapons necessary to win are as well, we will deal with spiritual things carnally.

In addition to the world and the devil, *we* can be our own enemy. When we accept ideas, philosophies, the condemnation, situations and opinions that are contrary to what God has spoken to us in His Word, we become our own enemies. Yes, the devil is real and is around us, but we could also be the one speaking death and curses in our lives.

That happens when we allow the enemy to create a mindset in us that is at odds with God's will and God's Word. This is what I was dealing with. The enemy attempted to influence my mind through fear of the unknown: a complete, no holds barred relationship with God.

As I matured, God's Word really began penetrating and transforming my spirit. When I heard the Word, I could see what God saw – a new me in Christ – convinced of the truth. I did not know how wonderful it would be and that it was not as hard as I thought.

I had been through so much in my own life that it was hard to trust that things would be better if I gave God all control. Crazy was everywhere, and I had a nice little set of guidelines on how to deal with it all. I knew how to not get hurt and how to not be affected by everything around me. I refused to be anyone's victim or fool and I believed that if I let God run things that He might let folks who violate me get away and leave me to nothing but prayer and humility. And, that just did not cut it for me.

I was afraid He would not be my avenging God (Romans 12:19) and that instead He would be the "we will love them through it" God and the "understanding" God and I was more concerned that the "sword and shield" God had my back.

I was hesitant since I did not know what God would do. I was scared to give into full submission. Scared of what would come from transformation. I was subconsciously operating in fear and allowing "crazy" to dictate to me. I was lying to myself about my false sense of security. I believed that my way was keeping me safe from crazy relationships and a crazy world with crazy people thinking they were sane when they were all crazy. I guess I was in that crazy boat myself. Crazy recognizes crazy.

But the Word was constantly working in me and slowly but surely I was becoming weary of my way. My choices were becoming different and life was getting easier.

After I graduated from college I began to work on me. God had begun a great work in me, and I was beginning to let His light shine brighter than my own.

I began to move forward and settle down. I ventured into friendships and even opened myself to dating just for fun - nothing more and nothing less. The most important new friendship was with a guy named Chris. He went from friend, to boyfriend, to fiancé and husband really fast.

Chris was and is such a sweet, solid guy. He was everything on my list, and I did not think there was anyone who fit *my* list! His integrity, his desire for truth and fairness was rare. I was attracted to his uniqueness, his clarity and individuality. He reminded me of all the good in myself that I liked and protected within me.

Over a year before I met Chris I regularly had three consecutive dreams every few weeks for about six months straight. In the dreams I would introduce a man to my family and we would marry, but I never saw the face of the man. His face was always a blur. I could only see around him and sense him and get a glimpse of the blur that was his face out of my peripheral.

The dream itself was unusual, not because I could not see this man's face, but because I had already decided that I would never marry. Consequently, when the dreams stopped, I thought no more about them.

About a month after Chris and I began dating the dreams returned, but the face belonged to Chris. It was startling because none of the others I dated ever popped up in my dream - just Chris. I had just met Chris. Wary, I tried to slow things down with Chris in case I was moving in a direction I did not want. Was this a warning? It did not matter. A few months later, Chris and I were engaged.

A year after Chris and I got married, I went to work for him at his construction company. It was great. But more crazies came out of nowhere - crazy for different reasons than before. I had never dealt with such viciousness, rumors, threats, hate. Then there were unhappy people seething with jealousy and envy. They needed someone to blame and chose us.

I worked hard at not getting offended, so it was a little rough for me at the start, but I got a handle on it. Chris was not bothered by it, so I tried to emulate my husband. Then, I started having physical issues - miscarriages - and sensitivity reared its head. Stuff just piled on. It was a trying time for both my husband and myself.

Chris and I tried for over a year to get pregnant. When we stopped trying, I got pregnant. But there was a miscarriage. Then, I was pregnant again. I went to a specialist after the first miscarriage, who refused to do any real testing. Why? I did not fit the profile for having any at-risk issues. All tests were normal and the doctor was going with that. On top of that, our health insurance did not cover the other tests.

I offered to pay for further testing but he was still insistent that it was unnecessary.

I switched to another doctor where many of Chris's family and a few associates were patients. He had a great nursing staff even though he had no personality, so I thought I'd stick with him. I thought - *if he's good, okay, I don't need him to love me.*

He was my doctor during the second pregnancy. I was so excited when I found I was pregnant again. After the ultrasound, I was informed there was an empty sac - I must have miscarried. He told me it appeared that something had been there, but not any longer. I was devastated.

On top of that, I had to continue taking blood tests to check hormone levels. I would have to have a D and C (dilation and cutery) to remove what was left of the pregnancy if it did not pass out of my body.     Since there was evidence of the pregnancy still left, my hormones were signaling that I was still pregnant. The blood tests would let the doctor know when hormone levels were decreasing and my body was rejecting what was left of the pregnancy. About a week later, I was called into the doctor's office because my hormone levels were still quite high and elevating. I went back in for an ultrasound and the sac was gone. Further observation showed there was another baby. I'd had twins. One I had miscarried and the other one was now stuck in my fallopian tube.

I saw the little heart beat and just fell to pieces. I was so excited, but was told that the baby had to be removed. It could not be saved. If I did not have the baby removed I would die. WHAT! After everything was explained I was crushed. I could not believe it. I had never even heard of this.

The doctor snapped off of his gloves, shrugged his shoulders and said – "Uh, no big deal, you just try again. It is so early, don't worry about it," and walked out.

I was left in shock. I thought, *did I just hear what I thought I heard? Did he just blow this off? This is the closest I've gotten to a healthy pregnancy, a baby - a child - and he tells me to blow it off. Did he honestly tell me to blow off the fact that I have to have a child removed from my body to die? Did he really encourage me to blow off the fact that my dream of being a mother is shattered again? Did this guy really just say no big deal? Who was this guy? Did he do this so often that he'd forgotten how devastating this is for a woman? Did I just experience a cold bedside manner?*

The nurses came in and sure enough, made up for the coldness, but I was done with this guy. I was nervous about the specialist to whom he referred me for the surgery. When he told me that they were friends, I thought, *birds of a feather flock together.* I did not know if I could deal with another doctor treating my situation as if it were not worthy of his attention.

I went to the specialist and he was unbelievable. Both he and his staff were God-sent. The surgery went well. I stayed in his care as long as needed. When he told me that I had to start going back to my regular doctor because I was no longer a special case I was devastated. His specialty was at-risk cases and now that I was "better" there was no need to see him anymore.

I asked for a reference to someone with a bedside manner like his, but he would not do it. He said that the other doctor was his friend, he was a great doctor and may have just been busy the times I met with him. He went on to explain how everyone is different.

That was a different I did not need from someone sticking his hands in me annually. So I was off again to figure things out and to look for a new doctor.

So much was going on that I was just plain tired. Tired of life. Tired of the hustle. Tired of the never-ending downs and the temporary ups. Even partying and living the high life was boring and usually ended with a headache. The challenges in my life were still there. After the weekends of excitement, the nights of entertainment and the trips, Chris and I would come right back to face those challenges all over again. The roller coaster ride, the coping and keeping our chins up were getting pretty old for me. My spirit was empty. My marriage and my family were great, but the emptiness was cavernous.

Life was caving in on me. A suffocating feeling would sometimes overwhelm me when I left the house Monday through Friday. Did I care too much about things that shouldn't matter? Yes! Day-to-day living overshadowed the recuperative process of the miscarriages and I did not deal with the impact of losing my babies. I just did not realize that I could not heal from and conquer what I did not confront.

I now understood women in the Bible like Sarah and Rachel and Hannah who thought they could not have children and it became a reproach. I felt as if my womanhood had been diminished. I am a female, I am supposed to have babies. Why can't I hold a pregnancy?

With that pressing on my brain, things loomed larger than they were. Situations were more dramatic, more devastating and more egregious. I did not know how to deal with my losses. My inability to handle what I'd gone through made me touchy and unenthused about things or people. I felt my nerves were danced upon regularly by everyone, though they did not know it. Folks were working my nerves and I did not know why. I get it now, but back then I just kept asking myself what was going on?

I was saying the right things. I spoke to myself regularly trying to convince myself I was fine. But I did not believe it and it did not make me feel better. There was no peace. There is peace only if we believe and trust the knowledge we hold. There is only peace if we trust the truth of God's Word. My pain was screaming so loud it overshadowed my ability to receive comfort.

So, I stopped and began to search for what I knew was best but had denied myself. I searched for truth in the Word of God. I searched to connect to Him Who had been calling me since I could remember. I began to read the Bible every day, listen to sermons, study, try to find peace and make sense of everything. I thought if I did not submit myself to God, if I did not stop living life on my own terms, God would allow me to be broken down to a place I did not want to go.

I got pregnant again. We had a beautiful little girl we named Madison and I stopped running and told God, "I submit myself to your call. God, I want you to use me. I want the best."

Right after that, I saw the changes in my own spirit. I opened myself to the Lord and began to have dreams and visions again, as I did when I was a child. Then a strange thing happened.

Chris, my husband, and I were in bed with our daughter Madison, and I awoke to Chris's muffled scream in his sleep. I asked him what happened but he would not say. I could tell he was disturbed, because he got up and did not come back to bed. I woke up later, after he'd gone to work.

I heard footsteps in our room. The dog was walking around the room, and though I could not see anyone, I felt a presence and sensed the dog following it. What was going on? The dog stopped on my side of the bed and stood.

*Something* sat on the bed, and the mattress felt as if it were being pulled from the bed. I tried to move and could not.

I tried to scream, but my mouth was paralyzed as well. I screamed, *the blood of Jesus, the blood of Jesus!* over and over in my head and then, "Jesus, Jesus, Jesus," I attempted to say it out loud. It was hard to move my mouth to say the entire phrase, so I just concentrated on calling Jesus. It was so hard to talk. Finally, I was able to get "Jesus," out of my mouth, and my mouth was free.

I pled the Blood again, over and over, and the mattress snapped back in place and I could move. I began praying over Madison and my husband. I called Chris to tell him what happened.

He said, "I don't know what's going on, but something sat on my side of the bed, and when it sat down, I felt my soul being pulled and I could not breathe. I was fighting something I could not see."

## Chapter 2

# *And Your Daughters Shall Prophesy*

*And it shall come to pass afterward that I will pour out My Spirit on all flesh; Your sons and your daughters shall prophesy, your old men shall dream dreams, your young men shall see visions. Joel 2:28*

RIGHT AFTER THE EPISODE IN the bedroom, I had three dreams over three consecutive days. All three dreams were disturbing and I knew there was something to the dreams because I could not stop thinking about them. They stayed in my spirit and on my mind all day long.

The first dream occurred July 19, 2006. In it, I was on vacation with my family along with a few other relatives, in-laws, and a couple of friends from the military. Somehow we got stuck in this Safari Camp with no transportation to leave. The vehicles used to drop us off were not functioning. Only one vehicle was able to make it back to get us. As many as possible filled up the autobus and left. The rest of us were going to wait until it returned. If it was not able to make it back that night due to the muddy conditions, we knew that the next morning a number of other autobuses would be available to come get us all.

We began cooking and preparing for the possibility of an overnight stay. While we were cooking, snakes began to show up around the campsite. They were everywhere. They leapt out of the trees. Snakes hung from the branches and launched strikes at us from every direction.

Awhile into the attack, I happened upon a way to kill them. This technique also gave us the ability to sense the snake's position and method of attack before it occurred. I was vehemently launching an attack on the snakes. The passion to go after them was so intense and second nature, I felt like a superhero in a movie.

I could feel the adrenalin rush. I feared what would happen if I did not give into the adrenaline and fight more than I feared what would happen in the fight. I looked. Snakes were everywhere.

As if in a trance, I focused on the attack. I stopped a moment, looked up and saw others around me about to be attacked. Some fought, and others ran while still others cowered under tables. It was raining snakes.

I yelled, "Kill them!" and "Stop running!" Everyone was scared. I knew why they were scared, but felt we could not give into the fear or we would never make it out. We had to hold on until the morning. It was already dark. Morning would not be long coming. I wanted everyone to fight and not fear, but the snakes' attacks were intensifying. They were not only landing on us, they were biting us. It was horrible.

Soon, I was one of the few left who were fighting. Everyone else was running or ducking from the snakes leaping and flying out of the trees over the campsite. They were exhausted as well as terrified. As the situation got under control and the snakes lessened, I ran to the others to show them how to kill the snakes using the new technique.

We used cookie sheets and garbage-can lids as our shields, and we had knife-like swords. I used the shield to cover myself as I charged and to deflect the falling snakes while slashing the slithering and jumping snakes with my knife.

I showed others how to use their peripheral vision and how to tap into their senses to anticipate a snake's move. That way, they would know whether to use the sword or the shield, be on the offensive, and take down more than one snake at a time.

I shared with them how to survive, stay protected, and make it through the night without being killed or bitten by the snakes, by working together.

The second dream was July 20, 2006. My husband Chris and I were watching television in our bedroom. Chris was about to turn off the television because the program had ended and the station was going off the air. You could hear the station announcer counting down the station's signal shutdown.

There was a clock with the hand going around the face, and in the center of the clock were numbers coinciding with the announcer's countdown. I was singing the alphabet and counting to my daughter Madison at the same time. She fell asleep on me during the counting, and Chris turned the television off with the remote.

When the television was turned off, I heard Madison speaking. I looked at her, and she was counting down where the television announcer left off. She said nine, ten, eleven, twelve, and thirteen—and then she stopped. I looked at Chris and asked if he had heard what I heard: Madison was counting in her sleep. He looked at me with an expression that said "what in the world?"

I replied to the look on his face and said, "Yeah that should be scary since she is so little, only a few months old, but maybe she will be a genius."

I looked up, the room shifted and I could tell I was dreaming. I looked at Chris again and laughed in response to the shifting of the room, realizing I was having a crazy dream. As I laughed, my left front tooth fell out.

The tooth was huge. I felt the space in my mouth with my tongue, but there was a tooth in the space. It was not empty. The tooth was a regular-size tooth. It was not huge like the one that fell out. I looked at Chris again and said, "What does this mean? I have never had a dream where I lost a front tooth or, when I did lose a tooth, another tooth took its place."

Then the second tooth, the regular-size replacement tooth, became loose and started to bleed out everywhere. I woke up very disturbed by the dream. I knew it meant death, but that's all I could be sure of.

The last dream was July 21, 2006. It was the most elaborate and detailed dream of the three. I went to the store, got some food, and took it back to the office. But the office was also a church and a house. I was getting out of the car, and a guy that I was familiar with, but did not remember who he was except that he worked for my husband walked up to me.

Even though could not make out his face, I felt there was a deep-rooted relationship between us. I sensed he was going through some things in his personal life. I could feel that he was hurting, but it made no sense to me at the time. After the dream, he was revealed to me. He was supposed to help me with the groceries, but instead, he kept hugging me.

I went to the backseat of the car to get my daughter Madison out of the car, but she was not in her seat. I thought perhaps I'd left her with my family. When I looked again, she was sitting in another seat. Confused, I turned around, and the man started hugging me again, patting my back as if he were comforting me.

I felt uncomfortable and confused about where I was, where my daughter was, who this guy was, and why he kept hugging me. I told him to get off of me and to get the groceries. I then reached in to get Madison to take her into the building.

I walked in the building, and my mother was standing in the living room our house. I told her there were groceries in the back of the car that I needed to get. She told some of the boys in the next room to go get them.

As I walked further into the house, I saw that not only were my brothers in the room, but my cousins as well. One cousin in particular that stood out was Vaughn. He stood out because he had neither been to my house, nor had I ever had a real relationship with him, since he was a younger male cousin. He also lived out of the country.

In the kitchen were all of my sisters, including my sister Vanessa, who had never been to our home and lived halfway across the country. At first I thought I was looking at my Aunt Vanessa, but it was fuzzy. I know now that it was my sister Vanessa, because since the dream, things have been revealed to me and the dream has come to pass (every one of the people in the house were at the funeral for Madison). In the kitchen were other relatives and in-laws. I was wondering what everyone was doing there.

Someone said something about getting ready, and we all got dressed to go to the space next door that was a church hall. We were still in the same building, but it was no longer the office or our home, it was a church reception hall. The room was set up for some kind of a reception.

I was not sure why we were there. I kept assuming it must be a family reunion or wedding reception. There were family members, in-laws, old friends, associates, and others I did not recognize visually, but felt a tie to. We were all sitting at long white tables eating or waiting to eat. Chris, Madison and I were sitting at the end of a table one row away from a backdoor. There were older people at the table behind us and children at the table next to them by the door. My aunt and uncle were sitting near us at a table, and I could make out my parents in the background of the room further away.

All of a sudden, the backdoor behind the table of the elders flew open, and a brown rhinoceros with a huge horn broke through. People were running, climbing on tables, screaming. The place was in chaos. Someone uttered, "it is a ram"; someone else shouted, "it is a buffalo!"

I yelled, "No, it is a rhinoceros." I went over to the door and picked up a chair and started whaling on it. I tried to beat it back out of the door and close the door at the same time. The thing passed out in the doorway, and I could not close the door. Everyone in the room was on top of tables, and the kids at the table near the door were still sitting at the table watching.

I shouted to no one in particular at the table next to the kids' table, "Pick up the kids, get the kids!"

No one moved. I hopped down off the table I was standing on and grabbed the kids one by one. I turned around, and there was a child walking toward me with another child in tow. He reached forward to hand me the child, and I picked them both up and passed them to someone near me who I thought would take care of them if anything happened.

Then an even larger rhinoceros came through the door and stepped over the one passed out in the doorway. He was massive, with an even larger horn on his nose and a scowl on his face.

He walked along the wall near the door and headed toward the aisle leading to the center of the room. My uncle was standing along the wall in front of the rhinoceros. He picked up something and was pounding the rhinoceros in the face the way I did to the first rhinoceros. I went over to help him. I thrashed the rhinoceros with a small table on the left rear side of the animal while my uncle was pounding him from the front.

I urged my uncle to try to beat the rhinoceros back toward the door. My uncle imparted a direct and deliberate smack across the rhinoceros's face. The rhinoceros was startled by the impact. He stopped advancing and shook himself. My uncle paused, and the rhinoceros gave my uncle a look.

My uncle froze in mid strike, and it was almost like the animal sent a chill through him. He was definitely unnerved. He then asked me to "just let the rhino in and let it do what it wants to do; it will leave on its own when it is done."

I said, "No, I am not letting it do anything with all of these people in here." Then the rhino turned to me and said, "Don't you know who I am?"

I answered, "I don't care who you are; you are getting out of here."

He replied, "If you put me out of here, you will regret it."

I responded back to him, "Oh, you are getting out of here!" He had the nerve to tell me he was offended. I let him know that I was not scared of him. "Everyone else might be scared, but I am not scared." I followed with an unrelenting beating to its head.

I got it backed against the door entryway. He fell to the ground, knocked out cold. A few seconds later, he got up and ran out of the doorway where the first rhinoceros was still laying.

After he exited the building, the first rhinoceros woke up and backed out of the doorway. I closed the door, and the heavy steel door transformed into a regular flimsy wood door with a screen. The locks on both the wood door and the screen door were rotted off, but the catch lock on the screen was still attached. So I closed the doors, locked the catch lock on the screen, and held the door closed with my body and arms stretched across the door.

The room was quiet, and the people were looking at me with a look that said, "You shouldn't have done that." They were paralyzed with fear from what the rhinoceros said. They were clutching each other, too frightened to get off of the tables. Not sure what to do, I began to speak to the room about having faith. I thought if I encouraged them, they would focus and rise to the occasion.

With tears flowing down my face and a mix of trepidation and empowerment in my chest, I cried out to the room, "How dare we not even have faith in the house of God! You have to believe we will be safe in the house of God, especially if we all pray. They want to destroy us, but they would have to destroy all of us. They can't do it if we don't allow them. It is us against them. We will be okay. Trust God! You have to try God to trust God and trust God to try God!"

I kept repeating it over and over while the tears streamed down my face. I was begging everyone to believe me, to trust God. I felt that if they did not trust with me, all of my efforts would be in vain, and whatever was coming on the other side of that door would destroy us all.

I wanted them to trust, not just for me, but for themselves, for the children most vulnerable in the room and the elderly who could not fight what was coming against us. I wanted us to be victorious and destroy whatever this rhinoceros was so that he would know who we were in Christ. I could not care less about who he thought he was.

I serve an awesome God, and I was not about to bow to this. He was not going to scare me. I refused to be afraid.

All of this was going through my head while a rumble was growing outside the door like a stampede coming closer and closer.

When I finished speaking, a boom came against the door and jolted me. It continued over and over. *Boom! Boom! Boom!* Each ram of the door got stronger and stronger, with only me holding the door. They were coming against the other side with such force that the brick wall around the door was shaking. The bricks were cracking and breaking apart, falling around me. I was holding the door closed, screaming and praying to God.

I could hear the voice of the larger rhinoceros speaking. I did not understand or remember what he was saying, but you could hear him. All the other animals were breathing loud and running back and forth in unison. The church hall was emptying out with every crash. People were running out of the front door, attempting to leave and escape whatever they thought was going to happen. We did not know what was on the other side, but we did know that the rhinoceros brought reinforcements to prove his point.

After awhile, the only people left in the building were me and my family. They did not leave, but they were all standing back near the front entry, waiting with apprehension. They never verbalized their concerns or desire to give in. They were praying and hoping with me.

All of a sudden, it just went silent, and the door ramming stopped. I waited for a moment to make sure it had actually stopped and was not a setup for something more.

I moved from the door toward my family on the other side of the reception hall. They were looking at me, alarmed at what had just happened. I scanned their faces, and instead of acknowledging their looks, I looked away and began to straighten up the room. Everyone else soon followed me in my action.

My aunt walked past me with her cane, and I spoke in a quiet somber whisper, turning my face slightly in her direction. "No one had faith. All those people in the church, and no one had faith. You know, faith comes by hearing, hearing of the Word. You strengthen that faith by trusting God. You have to try God to trust God and trust God to try God, and your faith will be strong. No one believed."

A sadness and disappointment fell over me so strongly. I realized no one really believed but me; I was at the door alone. All of those people in the church, and none of them believed enough in God to trust Him. None of them knew the Word enough to have faith in what they proclaimed to believe.

There was no understanding, no wisdom, and no relationship. There was no presence of the mind or spirit of God. I was alone in my belief. I did not understand why or how that could be. The answer to that was even more disheartening than the question itself.

As I began to walk away from her, my aunt turned her head toward me and agreed with what I said with a "yeah." As we cleaned up, a conversation ensued among my family about faith, God, and what had happened.

I continued to express astonishment at the situation by reaffirming my conclusion, "No one believed. No one believed." Over and over again, I murmured this.

Suddenly I was sitting at a table with a man I believed was my father and a couple of other family members. The table was located in the same room, but near a new door in the corner on a wall perpendicular from where the previous backdoor was located.

I was exhausted and still bewildered. The phone rang, and the man I believed to be my father answered the phone. He informed me that I had a call and told me I was to go pick up someone from an airport. I got up apprehensive, with little hesitation, and got my keys and purse. I don't remember who I was told I would pick up from the airport, but I knew when my father spoke, that that was what I was supposed to be doing.

When I walked through the new doorway to get to the stairs, my clothing changed. I now had on a white cream silk shirt and cream pants. The pants had a long decorative shiny belt with tassels at the end, and I had on long white pearls around my neck down to my knees. My clothes, my shoes, the belt, and the jewelry were all exaggerated in length or size. I struggled to walk down the stairs. I almost tripped over the belt and pearls. I felt awkward in my shirt and hunched over, trying to brace myself in preparation of a fall.

When I got to the bottom of the stairs, I noticed that I was at the bottom of the same outside stairway where I began the dream, but everything else outside was different.

My clothes fit different as well. My clothes, my shoes, the belt, and the jewelry all fit perfectly, and my hair was wonderful. I was stunningly gorgeous head to toe. I was glowing, calm, peaceful, and no longer tired or dazed. I began to strut to my car and noticed the parking lot was not the same one I started the dream in. It was a church parking lot, not the office parking lot.

There were also people standing near the street on my left. Many of them were the same people that ran from the church reception hall when the rhinoceroses were bashing the wall. Others were new faces. As I was walking to my car, I heard the people whispering and pointing.

Then I noticed an open field on my right, lined by trees on the right as far as the eye could see and a line of bushes on the left of this field. Between the bushes and the trees in the open field were dead sheep. They were all white, dirty, and lying on their backs with all four legs straight up in the air—dead stiff. There were people —women, men, and children—in front of the sheep in the church yard that were transformed into statues frozen in mid stride. Some of their faces I remembered running out of the hall. Others I did not know.

As I looked at this incredible sight, I heard God speak like loud thunder on a speaker system, "The rhinos were turned into sheep, and now they are all dead. This is what was trying to bust in. All of these animals tried to bust down that door, but your faith withstood all of this. Your faith saved them."

The sound was peaceful though booming. I stopped for a second and thought about what I'd heard. I was taking it in, making sure I did not miss anything and did not misinterpret anything. I repeated what I heard and then said to myself, "Oh, my goodness, my faith saved them, my faith saved them in the room? Even though they did not believe and they did not stand with me, my faith was all I needed?

I looked up and noticed the sun was shining bright. The sky was clear and blue; the grass and trees were deep green and perfect in every way. It was a beautiful day, and more people began to gather along the parking lot and along the road. I could overhear people saying, "Did you hear about what happened?"

"This is what is left of what happened."

"This church did this."

"That church is something."

"They did this."

"They stopped this."

The people along the road were taking pictures of the sheep and the statues of individuals. More and more gathered. Whenever someone would stop, the word was passed to them of the occurrence and present resulting event before us. While I walked to the vehicle, I recalled the voice of God and what He'd said.

I smiled and bubbled over with joy and said to myself, "My faith did this. My faith stopped this from coming in. My faith saved us from this."

I opened my truck, and my camera was in the passenger seat. When I reached for it, I woke up.

After these dreams, I called my father, who is a pastor and has the gift of interpreting dreams. I told him the dreams. It was obvious from his silence and his groan every now and then that he was somewhat disturbed. The end was the only thing that gave him any comfort.

We discussed certain parts of the dream that I now know to have been about the illness and death of my daughter. The part where my tooth fell out, the part where the rhinoceros came in, the feeling of loss in the dream, the part where Madison was in the car and then was gone and then in a different seat and side of the vehicle. The counting to thirteen. The dream within a dream. These are all signs of death, passing to the other side, a disturbance and attack in one's life or spiritual walk.

The dream within a dream meant a message within the message, a prophecy. I kept asking if he thought it was my daughter Madison and if she was going to die or was she used as a symbol for someone or something else. Sometimes dreams are literal and other times a person is used as a symbol for another person close to you who is alike in personality, mannerisms or it could be a symbol for yourself. A symbol of a part of yourself that is being dealt with or exposed. The best advice on dreams: ask God for the interpretation. Some things must come to pass and others can be stopped through prayer and action.

I think Dad wanted to believe that it would be someone else. Neither of us wanted her—not our miracle—to suffer anything, let alone die. He refrained from answering and told me he had to pray about it and would get back to me.

He always called her "Praise." He would say every time he saw her that she was to bring praise. She was purposed for praise, he would say. I don't think even he knew just how deep and how true that would be or all that would come with that praise and purpose. About a week or two later, I asked him about it, and he said he was still waiting and would get back to me on it.

I never pressed him about it again, hoping it did not mean anything, but wondering if he knew more than he was saying and how bad was what he knew. He usually answered immediately if I asked him about a dream. Even if it were something really intricate, within days it would be clear to him.

I know his gift can be heavy at times and it scares folks when he can tell them things revealed to him through dreams, their dreams as well as his. I know it is also a weight to him when dreams are presented to him that prophesy things he would rather not know or deal with, which tells of upcoming pain or loss.

I remember asking him about the spirit of prophecy and a dream I had about the prophetic and his answer told me a lot. He said, just because you know something doesn't mean you are to say anything. If it is not for the glory of God you need to pray about what to do with the information. Just because you know, doesn't mean you are to say anything. I thought to myself, what a burden, to know something that is going to happen, but you can't say anything because the person or persons involved cannot handle it. At times the knowledge of what is to be cannot change the realities already established in the spirit. How do you deal with the burden of knowledge about another long before they carry the burden, before it is manifested in the earth?

Revelation before manifestation can be arduous to even those who claim to be sound in their understanding and spiritual existence. I would leave it alone, for his sake and mine. I pretty much knew there was something yet to come that I did not care to know or want to face.

I am not sure if he even remembers those dreams. I never asked him about them again and other things happened right after causing me to forget until I read my diary when I was in the hospital with Madison. I think he forgot about it as well. I have still not asked him about them. When I reread the dreams in the hospital, I knew I did not want to know anything about the dreams except the end. I knew the end was good.

I wanted to wait and see, not know and see. The last thing my dad told me to do when I asked him about the dreams was to write down all the dreams. So I wrote the dreams down. He then told me to pray and he was going to pray and that is what I did, I prayed and left it alone.

## Chapter Three

# By the River Chebar

*I know all the things you do, that you are neither hot nor cold. I wish
you were one or the other! But since you are like lukewarm water, I
will spit you out of my mouth! You say, "I am rich. I have everything
I want. I don't need a thing!" And you don't realize that you are
wretched and miserable and poor and blind and naked. I advise you
to buy gold from me—gold that's been purified by fire. Then you will
be rich. And also buy white garments so you will not be shamed by
your nakedness. And buy ointment for your eyes so you will be able
to see. I am the one who corrects and disciplines everyone I love. Be
diligent and turn from your indifference. (Rev. 15–19)*

I WAS NOT A WILD child. For the most part, I've always
been a pretty conservative person. However, where God
was concerned, I was really lukewarm. I just went to
church, paid my tithes now and then and tried to keep the
commandments – I just existed.

I was and wanted to be comfortable and did not want
waves in my life. I did not want to confront anything, deal
with anything or any hurt. I wanted to skate through life.
I had already seen enough through everyone else's pain and
turmoil.

To experience what was necessary for me to grow in my
spiritual life was not my desire. I was warped in my thinking
and believed that if I did not get too deep into and attached

to this life, the enemy would not come against me. Yeah, right.

I did not understand at the time that before I was born, God knew me and established me according to His purpose (Jeremiah 1:5). I did not understand that He created my beginning and my destiny and that it was in my best interest to complete my path to fulfill His plan.

I did not understand that although I had choices along the way, one way or another, I was going to get to His appointed destination for me. I did not understand that He already knew what I would and would not do and He had a remedy for that. I did not understand that He would call attention to my true path and away from my fear and confusion. He loved me and perfected me in His image and Spirit before I was even formed in the womb. Before people, ideas, and life touched what He had put inside me.

I was running away from my purpose, because to birth it meant labor pains. I did not want to think about the joy and the fulfillment afterward. I focused on that one page I had to get through in order to finish the story. I let the enemy trick me, telling me his way was easier, better, more fun, hassle free—and I believed it for a while.

I was walking away. I did not want to fight for what was promised by God. Before I was created in the earth, prosperity, success, love, patience, peace, kindness, and completeness were all mine, but I did not want to endure the walk. Though I know now that anything worth having is worth fighting for, in my young eyes it did not seem that way because I saw so many losing their battles. Struggling to stay in the fight. *Why are they trying so hard to end up just a bit ahead?* I would ask myself.

It just did not seem worth the fight. It appeared that those who just went with the flow were doing fine. What I did not realize is that everyone chooses their own path—

their way or God's way. Whether we follow God or not is between us and God. I can't do what someone else does and use them as my reason for not doing God's will. We choose the way with our decisions.

Had I paid more attention to the ones who were flowing, I would have recognized the signs of their unhappiness; they had no real peace, and so they partied and did everything to fill the emptiness. They were trying to fill a void that God only could fill. But they were too busy running. Money, casual relationships, material gains, and all the outward signs of success and happiness did not afford them peace; there was no real love and no goodness—and much regret and confusion.

They were constantly on the move and involved in things because if they stood still long enough, they would hear themselves think, and their God-given consciences would speak. They might acknowledge their sins and need for God.

The music must be loud, the parties must be wild, and life must be exciting and fast, because if it quiets or slows down, truth will set in. We are afraid of the truth of who we are and the power of God which should be at work in our lives.

How can I be everything God is calling me to be? How can I do all the things God wants me to?

The children of Israel asked: *Can God prepare a table in the wilderness? Behold, He struck the rock, So that the waters gushed out, And the streams overflowed. Can He give bread also? Can He provide meat for His people?* (Ps. 78:19–20)

It is amazing how quickly our faith wanes and we put faith in man's failing hands, seek counsel based on misguided principles and institutions established on greed, frailty, and selfishness which take away any power and authority we could possess. Then we question God and His ability to do what He says and fulfill His promises. Yet, our survival and His goodness in spite of us speaks volumes to His existence, presence and power.

At around twelve or thirteen years old, I watched my mother hurt because life was such a burden. She'd never admit it, but I knew more than she cared for me to know. I knew she was carrying a load in spite of her loving and engaging spirit. I often watched how she handled life. I watched her because I was a female and she was my future— woman, wife, mother, girlfriend, sister. I believed that she would tell me who I was and would be. I related to her and I internalized her.

But I saw life wearing on her. Some days were better than others, but it was still a constant strain to move forward. The strain of keeping up with bills and paying for everything we kids were involved in or needed impacted her greatly. Making sure we were healthy, happy and protected was a 24/7 job.

There was always something going on. Mom and dad were trying to figure it out for themselves and for their children at the same time—and the thought of getting up to do it all over again each day was enough to put anybody right back in the bed.

Being married, managing finances and life were not principles passed down through the family. You figured it out on your own, because the generation before did not talk about those things. Adults and children did not share those kinds of issues. Especially not church folk. It was not proper. Everybody stayed in his place.

On the other hand, this was also a new day for my parents. My parents were learning to live with a freedom never possessed by their ancestors for over four hundred years. There was no preparation or instruction sufficient for my parents' generation that taught them how to properly utilize this newfound freedom. Survival—that's what they learned. Everything else was trial and error.

Eventually, they found their footing, but listening to and watching this young couple intently as they grew up in front of my young eyes, I came up with my own conclusions. True or not, my assumptions were imprinted on my immature spirit. Though I had a discerning spirit, I had yet to ascertain the wisdom of God; at that young age, I relied on my own understanding.

I saw my mom stretching money and faith just to make it another day—and without losing her mind. My mom worked two jobs, giving her all to God and the church, and still it did not seem enough. Maybe the yoke she shouldered just happened to be in her life at the same time I was more intensely watching the woman after whom I was patterning myself. Whatever the reason, I saw the hardship and it hurt me to the bone.

To be perfectly honest, included were all the women around her as well. The women at church, the women she worked with ... her sisters. In their conversations, they lightened their burdens with jokes and stories that were always rhythmically chided with an "uh-huh" or "I know what you mean, chile" or "ooh, yeah, Lord have mercy!"

As a child, I did not see the humor or understand the relief in knowing that they understood one another's pain. I was actually quite saddened that this was not unusual and that possibly behind all the smiling faces of the women I adored and dared to one day be like was the same quality of life and its cruelties.

The pressure in my head and the tightening in my chest at this revelation was too much. *If this is how it felt as a child, who doesn't herself bear the burden, how much more when I grow up and I am her?*

My father's burden was heavy as well, but a girl doesn't pay as much attention to Daddy as she does to Mommy. Most fathers, like mine, did not wear life on their faces or sleeves. Men usually keep a poker face. I had not yet developed the ability to read males. Women are different - it is easy for one female to read another female. Besides, my mother was my field of study.

This little girl went into her room feeling hopeless because I knew no amount of being good, cooking or cleaning for her, or anything else I could do would take that weight from her. I just cried. I cried, and I made a decision that day that I did not want to live past twenty-one. I changed it because I remembered so many reminiscing about their twenties. So, I said I just did not want to make it to thirty, where it hurts like that. Maybe I would leave here in the heyday of my twenties.

I made a conscious decision: *if You don't answer this prayer, God, because it is not Your will, then I just want to coast through this life and get it over. I don't want to feel it because seeing it is too much already.*

Over time I developed a very nonchalant attitude about this life. The problem with that is when I loved, I loved hard and deep down inside wanted to love everybody. I was always able to find something good in everything and everyone.

But you can't be nonchalant and love at the same time. You can't walk in love and turn off love at the same time. You can't walk away from who you are and believe things will work out. You then become a contradiction and promote instability in your own life because of your own double-mindedness.

When I did have friendships or relationships outside of my family, this double mind-set caused me to attract people who could not love me back. They themselves were double-minded and did not love or embrace or even know who they truly were in this life.

They thought they loved me, but because they did not love themselves, they could not love anybody else. They could not be faithful and could not be truthful. I did not have much more spiritually, but they wanted what I did have because it was still more than what they possessed within themselves.

I may not have wanted to walk in the anointing, but God's presence was always there due to the prayers of those who loved me and the covenants established by God with those before me. Outsiders saw it. They saw the inner me and even called me out. But I still denied it as if doing so would make it so.

Instead of confronting and dealing with my self-made life and my self-destructive life, I created a new principle I thought would thicken the cover: I decided to make myself completely uncaring and to only care about me and what was important to me. I told myself that it was not the people that bothered me, but their rejection and their inability to love me the way that I wanted them to.

I told myself it was the rejection and not the life I was creating that was a magnet for negativity. I thought the rejection from God, from people, from life, from my dreams, from my hopes was what was hurtful, and so out of the imagination of my mind I rolled with that. It was everyone else - that was the problem because they would not conform to me and my needs.

I thought I could fix everyone and not care. You can roll my way or roll on out of my face. I was in a mode where whatever happened, my response was, "Such is life, let's move on and don't deal with it. Move away from it, and it will not matter."

I admit that it felt sort of freeing not to care or become attached too often. But it was a falsehood and contradiction to who we are as the beings God created. We have to care about those that love us as well as those who don't, because we are love, created and birthed in love. It is sad that it is what we know best and yet walk away from the easiest. Why? Because love is patient, love is kind, love is giving, love is selfless, and all of that—and we don't want that. We want fast, hard, no pain, and it should be like Burger King and be made our way all the time or we want our money back.

What's worse is that I did not understand that rejection is a part of the birthing to new levels in life. You must be rejected and ejected from a thing or a place in order to transition to another place, a new place, the next stop on your journey. Rejection is not all bad. It is the end of one thing and the beginning of a new thing, a better thing. It is necessary change that increases and elevates us. I outgrew certain things, certain people, certain ideas. At some point, I got distracted and stuck in the negative side of rejection resulting in low levels of God-chasing and low self esteem.

I really did not understand God's process of transformation. I took rejection as a slight to who I was and not as a movement of God that was designed to lead me into who He destined me to be. I began to build on a false foundation and thought I could fool the rest of the world and eventually convince myself I was okay with what I really did not understand. I lacked the knowledge to assist myself in pin pointing how I was okay or what I was rejected from or into. I have since acquired this ability and learned that rejection was a necessary part of the transformation process on my journey.

I remember asking a friend of mine if he thought I had low self esteem. He was adamant and insisted that I had the highest esteem of anyone he knew. I had bouts of doubt every now and then, but low self esteem was definitely not on my list he explained. I thought about what he said and took it for what it was.

Well, I believed in myself, I valued myself and my self worth. I did not play games, did not like foolishness or drama, and desired only the best. I had self respect and high expectations, but I could not say definitely that ruled out low self esteem, despite the stigma attached to it.

There are CEO's, public officials, church leaders, heads of states, leaders, entertainers and the like who struggle with low self-esteem. Wealth, power and fame do not change this fact. In fact, low self-esteem may have been the driving force behind their accomplishments in an attempt to convince themselves they have self-worth or that they too are okay.

Those that have low self esteem act in response to the care of what others think about us, their rejection or acceptance of us and we question what their rejection or acceptance means about us. This can cause us to change, and not for the better. Someone's like or dislike of us can take precedent over the truth and the thoughts of the Most High about us.

Low self esteem is a consequence of operating in the low level of God chasing. Our spiritual relationship is shallow and therefore has no roots. With no root we are not firm in the knowledge of who we are and the lack of knowledge causes peril and grasping for ways to feel solidly planted where we know we are not. The fear that our roots are exposed and others will see and take advantage of that fact causes us to react or care about others opinions.

We often think that having low self esteem means we lower our standards and do crazy things to get others to like us, but that is not always true. Many do the opposite and go in protect mode and overcompensate. I would overcompensate in order to make myself feel safe in a world

I did not trust to love me back or keep me safe. This side of low self esteem leads us into building a self centered, self protectionist existence that is the foundation for fear and every other sin. The enemy will trick us into being alone. God said it was not good from man to be alone, because life then becomes about him and he is now self centered. He becomes the personification of sin, he misses the mark and is now ambiguous and contrary to God who has no self centeredness in Him. You cannot operate in the Spirit of God if you do not walk in the Spirit of God in accordance with His Word. Therefore, you cannot fulfill purpose.

Every human being will have times of doubt, but when we begin changing things about ourselves - changing jobs, changing looks, not because it is time to grow up or move on for better, but because we want acceptance of others, can't handle criticism or rejection or because we are uncomfortable about who we are and the decisions we make, we can be sure we are entertaining low self-worth.

I was not in a place that would allow me to walk in His ways. I did not understand what it meant, to be in His image and likeness, and that operation in such a power alone would keep me, not the power of my hands or the imaginations of my mind outside of His truth, His Word. The foundation of sand on which I built my philosophy of—*it is what it is, and I am not putting into this life more than I am willing to lose* — drew me to like-minded and like-spirited people and was a burden that I would later admit to. I did not want to care about or commit to this life, but I wanted someone else to care about and commit to me.

Even more, I did not understand that words are powerful and become reality and are a reflection of my heart and its dysfunction or its order (Luke 6:43-45). I thought about and spoke about rejection and disappointment and it became reality for me. I attracted like-minded people into my life

– kindred spirits. I expected everyone to be the same and they were because I put folks in boxes, told them to dance to a beat and then said – "Aha! I knew you would dance." Now that's crazy.

It makes no sense now, but back then I had rationalized it to make sense. In Psalm120:3, David writes about the deceitful tongue. We have to watch our own imaginations and how we speak and deceive ourselves into believing what is not true and not based on God's Word. I spoke death into my life and I attracted dead people. So now I was in relationship with dead people, causing more drama and turmoil. Exactly the thing I *did not* want to do. They wanted me to give them life and love, but I could not give what I did not have.

I was just as lost as they were. All I had were the prayers and protection of those who had come before me and the Word in my heart, which kept me safe. But having fallen among life's thorns, the Word was being choked because I largely disregarded God's Word, not fully realizing that only what is based on God's Word will last. Whatever is based on God's Word will stand in the storm. There was no song in my spirit, no song in my life.

*There on the poplars we hung our harps, for there our captors asked us for songs, our tormentors demanded songs of joy; they said, "Sing us one of the songs of Zion!" How can we sing the songs of the LORD while in a foreign land?* (Psalm 137:2)

## Chapter Four

# Until the Day Breaks

*Sacrifice and offering You did not desire; My ears you have opened. Burnt offering and sin offering You did not require. Then I said, "Behold, I come; In the scroll of the book it is written of me. I delight to do Your will, O my God, And Your law is within my heart." (Psalm 40: 6–8)*

I WAS RAISED ON THE Word of God. It was planted in my heart, but I lacked real understanding. What I should have gotten from watching my mother was her ability to walk in faith in the Word. God's anger with the newly delivered Israelites from Egypt was that they did not mix the Word with faith (Hebrews 4:1-5). Her faith was expressed in her tenacity - she never gave up, and God sustained us and took care of us and we never wanted for anything. All our needs were met, and whatever came against us, God took care of it.

Even with the so-called "deep" revelations, I was still a child and I thought as a child. I had seen enough to not want to fulfill my purpose, but I knew too much and had seen too much of God's power and greatness to not love God and deep inside I did desire what He had for me.

I say *love*, but I really did not love Him because to love God means to trust Him and to obey Him. I really loved the idea of God. Loved the idea of loving Him and Him loving me back in that great powerfully spiritual Father and child way.

I loved His promises, but not His process. I loved just pieces of Him, but not Him in His entirety. I loved the good and happy parts. The journey to good and happy? Not so much.

I did, however, want a relationship with Him that would put me at peace - where I knew the mind of God and could honestly live with a carefree attitude based on faith and truth, without the sweat. I would learn later everything has a price. The price would be time spent in God's Word, time spent *with* God, time soaking in the Holy Spirit and just time. It takes time and experience with God to discover that He is true to His Word. The truth of God's Word must be experienced in application to our lives. We must discover for ourselves that God's Word is true. And again, that only comes as we read God's Word, allowing its power to be activated in our lives.

My fear was that God's will might not be *my* will. Then what? There is always that fear that God's will just might turn out to be a desolate place and heaven will be the only thing worth looking forward to because there's nothing on earth for us. Right? Wrong.

This uninformed, distorted view has diverted a lot of those who could have been redeemed a long time ago. Not knowing God or His Word the way I should have, I did not know the truth of God. I knew the truth of men and confused souls professing God.

I knew about people preaching the theology of excuses for why the power of God was not present in their lives and why they were not moving on God's timeline. God's process is not the problem; we are.

*My people are destroyed from lack of knowledge. Because you have rejected knowledge, I also reject you as my priests; because you have ignored the law of your God, I also will ignore your children.* (Hosea 4:6)

Condemnation, excuses, fear, distortions, ignorance was marketed from the pulpit and Sunday school class, and the "poor me" syndrome became my birthright. I believed what I heard over the Word and over my own parents because these were the experts in the pulpit with all the titles.

In turn, I feared God—not out of love, but out of simple respect for His power and all the fearful things I'd heard about Him. Everyone was consistent in confessing His power and punishment. They emphasized the fear factor more than anything else. Everything that was not right was blamed on the devil or God's wrath. The devil's power seemed larger than God's and God's hate for my sin seemed greater than His love. But such distorted fear hurts and hinders instead of saves and heals. I would wonder often - Where is the love? Can a sister please get some love?

My perception of God created fear, doubt, confusion, and the inability to grow. I failed to do the work of digging (in His Word), transforming (allowing His Word to change my thinking), changing (matching my behavior with my new way of thinking), crying (in repentance for my stubbornness), stretching (faith to faith and glory to glory), and being who I was created to be.

Through all of this, I never stopped going to church or lessened my efforts for a better understanding. I went to church almost every Sunday. I use to go for the singing and praise, but things were changing and I was now waiting in anticipation for the Word to be preached. I was trying to make sense of it all. Slowly it was becoming clear. The love of God, His Holy Spirit began to shine brighter than all the other stuff and began to draw me near. God's forgiveness, His resurrection power, His love became real for me. I was filled with what I was hearing.

I thirsted for God, for His ways, and for the new me in Christ to be unleashed. I wanted to be in relationship with the Holy Spirit and understand His purpose for me. Then came one of those "aha" moments. I began to ask God for wisdom and understanding and the Word of God began to make sense in relationship to my life. After years of living disconnected, I totally surrendered to God and now it made sense. It dawned on me that fighting was harder than surrendering. I had only prolonged the inevitable, and God in His foreknowledge knew it. He was waiting on me to get it.

God was really helping me dredge out the lies from my pool of life. He was bringing clarity and focus to me. Bringing back to my remembrance all He had spoken over me, the greatness and blessedness that existed in me and that was laid out before me.

One of the major turning points in my life happened the year before I met my husband right before I began having dreams of marriage. I was partying with my cousins and drinking (not water) on New Year's Eve. We were in the driveway of my aunt's home. Most of the cousins decided to go in the backyard and shoot into the air, as they often do in many areas of Illinois, even now. I was not a fan of the gun-at-a party thing, so when they went in the back to shoot, I went in the front to sit in the car and stay warm and safe. We were getting ready to go to a club, so I pretended I was in a hurry and wanted to sit in the car while they did their thing. (I may have been crazy, but not stand-around-and-shoot-while-people-are-drinking crazy).

While I was sitting there, a couple of the other females came to the front and sat in the car with me to talk. We had the radio on and began counting down with the radio. We screamed and laughed and hugged and kissed each other. We were just excited to all be together for this time. It had been years - since we were kids - that we were together for New Year's. We were either all in college or married with children. It was wonderful just being together.

The guns started going off, and I began to pray that no stray bullets would come in our area and that everyone shooting in the backyard would be protected. And then God spoke. He told me to pray for change and a difference in my life this year. God convicted me concerning everything my cousins and I were previously laughing and talking about a little while ago—the carefree Godless life we were living—to repent of it all and make a change. He was convicting my spirit on the fact that here we were, pastor's children, grandchildren, and great grandchildren, acting like the masses. Oh, Lord. I was sitting here drinking, thinking about stray bullets, and now I was having a come-to-Jesus moment.

So I did what I was told, and in the backseat with a cup full of liquor on my way to a club, I prayed. Yes, the Holy Spirit showed up on New Year's night at midnight. I was hoping that no one would open the car door so the light would not come on, and that no one would turn the music down to hear me in the back crying and praying like I was on the altar at church.

He was speaking resurrection, bringing back life into the dead walk I called life and altering my path according to His Will and His Word. The rest of the night was crazy. I did not drink anymore, but I was still me, still buzzed, but convicted in my spirit. I kept thinking, here I am at the club trying to have a good time, but God showed up before I got here and changed all of that. I was not going to have an easy free time.

I was heavy with conviction. Every time I had a minute to think the Holy Spirit dealt with me. Yes, in the club on New Year's Eve I had a guest I was not expecting: the Holy Spirit. Try to break it down on the dance floor all night long with Him right there. It was not easy. I am sure it was not meant to be.

When I left and went back to school, I got rid of some friends, moved forward on some things, and began making a lot of changes in myself and around me. The brother-in-law of the man who would be my husband had been trying to connect us together for years. I decided that I would meet him, since I was going to a training that was in his area of the state.

I let him know that it must be understood that I was in a place of transformation and I did not want a relationship, I was not having relations, and I had not converted my tongue quite yet and would go off on him if he did not respect what I had laid out and he tried to test me.

His brother-in-law laughed and said, "That is why you guys have to meet; you are both so picky and think you are so special."    What was really funny was that I had just realized a few months earlier what he realized long ago after he first met me. I was picky and thought I was special, but now I knew it was not because of who I was per se, but because I realized the God in me and His blessing on my life.

I looked back over my life and realized that God was always there. He kept me and granted me favor in everything. Though I was not perfect in my ways, I prayed every day about almost everything and He answered. I read the Bible regularly, not consistently but regularly, and always went to church. Wherever I was, I found a church.

It was my own guilt and self-condemnation that the enemy played on to get me to destroy myself and turn me away from God's plan. He had me thinking I was disconnected, but I was always connected. God had shown Himself to me all my life, protecting me, not because I was so great, but because I belonged to Him and I had a purpose to serve in His kingdom on this earth and through that greatness would manifest. He has never left me nor forsaken me even in my sin.

I was on a better path, but there was still a lot of work God needed to do in me. Before the age of thirty, I submitted myself to further cleansing and transformation to bring more maturity and integrity within me so that God could establish His purpose on the earth through me.

What was cute at thirteen or even at twenty-three is no longer cute or beneficial at thirty. I needed God to make me what I needed to be.

One of my many steps was to accept me as God accepted me—mistakes, messed-up past, imperfect present and hope-filled future me. Good and bad me, crazy and intelligent me, emotional and cold me, overly positive and judgmental me, gregarious and shy me. All of me. No matter what part of me shines or dims during the day, God loves me—and now, so do I.

I wanted to be there. On fire. Purified. Cleansed. Clothed by the Holy Spirit. Blessed with the eye-opening anointing of Jesus. I wanted to be whole. No longer miserable and faking joy. No longer did my happiness hinge on the state of the moment.

Even His discipline is for my good because of His great love for me. It stings, but it doesn't hurt, because it is His love and always, *always works* out for my good. I could survive through all things—not because I wanted to—but because I knew in the end I would be victorious.

God already had ordered my steps. When He made me, knowing my end and everything in between, He placed inside me the ability to identify, confront, and conquer what is not from His Spirit.

I had a desire to connect to God Who is the Great I Am. We all, at some time, have failed to connect to the Most High God and instead connect to anything we perceive to be greater than us - things, people, drugs, sex, alcohol, ideas - whatever our other gods might be. And we stumble.

I already had the power to win – His Name is Jesus. I had to accept and believe it and apply it with the help of the Holy Spirit of God. I had to step into my breakthrough.

## Chapter Five

# And the Shadows Flee

*You are my hiding place and my shield; I hope in Your word*
*(Psalm 119:114).*

THE PEACE OF GOD WAS growing in my life. I was coming
to that place of rest and confidence. The more I dealt with
the baggage of my past and proclaimed the blessings of
my future, the better I got and the better everything and
everyone around me became. I unloaded and cleaned out
the things I picked up on the way that impacted who I was
and how I related to others.

I dealt with the baggage of past relationships so I would
not bring what others did or said into my marriage. I did not
want to act out what I had seen in other relationships, where
the husband or wife is constantly paying for the mistakes of
a previous occupant.

I worked on exchanging the library of information I
operated out of, which was full of contortions, fabrications,
distortions, and drama written by individuals and my own
ideologies. I wanted peace and truth. In order to have that, I
had to close the door on condemnation, fear, offense, strife,
and confusion because those are spirits in which God does
not abide. They are roadblocks to abundant living. They
block the blessings we pray for, fast for, sow seed for.

We think God is not answering our prayer, when the truth is that we are not clear to receive according to His principles and established ways. I put all of the unwanted stuff in a box and put a lock on it with a bow because I was happy to get rid of it. Once I became free, I realized that the spirits from those falsehoods were more of a burden than I thought.

I dealt with the loss of my children along with all of the other things in my library and I was pregnant with twins again. It was great. Everything seemed perfect. My mother flew in to see me since I was not flying home for the holidays. I was so excited to shop with her and do the things you do with your mother and talk about the things you talk about with your mother when you are having your first child. I was a little over five months pregnant. Over the weekend I got really tired and felt funny. I laid down and slept an entire day away. I thought the working and getting ready for twins must have worn me out and the next day I was fine.

My mother went home and a few weeks later I went to my ultrasound exam. Something happened at the last minute and Chris was running behind and could not make the appointment. I told him not to worry about it, I would get photos. I did not want to reschedule the appointment since it was going to be a quick routine exam.

I went in for the exam and I could see one baby really moving and the other one not so much. Just kind of floating. The ultrasound tech moved quickly away from the baby floating and went back to the one moving. Her face and tone changed. She took on an artificially jovial tone in the conversation. Her attempt at normalcy was not achieved. She tried, but her awkwardness was louder than her conversation.

I asked her, "is something wrong with the baby, did the baby die?"

She looked at me kind of shook up and stood up and said, "I have to go, the doctor is coming, I will be right back." I smiled a half smile because I already knew.

I laid back and told myself, "You can make it. If there is something different about this child or if it is dead, you can make it." I closed my eyes and tears fell. I took a deep breath and heard the doctor on the other side of the door.

She came in with her usual smile, but eyes saying something else. She then sat down in front of the screen.

We did the usual greeting and she said "Now, let's get a look at these babies."

I knew she was trying to keep things normal in case the technician was wrong. She went over a few things and then reached out for my hand.

"I have to tell you...."

I interrupted and said, "I already know, just tell me what I need to do from here. What does this mean?"

She gave me that look of sadness and relief and began explaining things to me and telling me how usual this unusual thing happens. Not to worry. She showed me a close up of the baby with its arms and legs folded over its body as if it laid itself to rest. She went further and showed me the fluid that collects at the crown of the head when a baby dies.

When the ultrasound light hits the head of a deceased baby, the fluid glows and it looks as if the baby has on a halo. She went on to explain his halo and how this beautiful little boy was now an angel. Then we went over the baby still living and I focused on her. I told myself she was alright and I cannot lose focus on her account. I could not be sad or frustrated because she would feel what I felt and I did not want that.

I was surprised to find that nothing is done during a multiple pregnancy when a child dies in utero and another baby is still alive and appears healthy. I had to carry the dead child all the way to the end of the pregnancy.

About two months later. The pressure of the live child (the baby girl) caused the sack of the baby boy (the deceased baby) to break and triggered labor. For hours I was in labor trying to push him out, the doctor tried pulling him out, but because he was so small and fragile, basically decaying in my body, they were afraid to pull too hard and snap his neck leaving his head inside of me and his body pulled off. This would lead to infection and other issues.

They were determined to keep the baby girl in as long as possible to bring her full term. I was only a little over seven months pregnant. They decided to leave him in and they focused on stopping the labor.

Once I was stable I was admitted to the hospital. For weeks I lay there - an oven waiting for my bread, my daughter, to finish baking while the doctors monitored me closely to make sure nothing happened. Making sure I did not get an infection and die in the process.

One evening I went to the bathroom and felt something between my legs. I reached down and felt an arm. The little boy was being forced out by the growth of the little girl. I called the nurse, she called the doctor and Chris came in right when they decided to take me to labor and delivery. Once again, all night they tried to get this baby out without interfering with the other baby. She still had about four more weeks before she would truly be full term. To no avail they decided to go ahead and do a C-section. The next day at eleven in the morning I was scheduled to have Madison. She was born at 11:15 am with her brother attached to her sack. He was absorbing himself into her placenta. That is why it was so hard to get him out.

He no longer looked like a baby so the doctor told me that she could not show him to me. She told me about him. Then the hospital set up a hospital burial and had a memorial set up for him at the hospital as they did with all of their losses.

When I named my daughter Madison Annon, it was a conscious decision. Annon was a name God put in my spirit two years before I was pregnant with her. I later decided to name her Zoe Annon because I always loved the name Zoe. When we lost Madison's twin in my fifth month of pregnancy, my husband and I went over names again because he sensed the baby to be born was not Zoe. We went with Madison, but we both believed Annon was to be part of her name. Her name means *son of Matthew*—Madison. And *giver of life*—Annon. She did exactly what she was called to do ... gave us life.

I could not believe that after everything, I finally had a child. I was ecstatic when they told me I was going home, until they told me Madison could not go. She was not gaining weight and they did not know why because she was routinely eating. I was so broken hearted. I did not want to go home without her and I did not want to hear about any issues.

About a week later, things changed. They asked us to spend the night in the hospital before we took her home and they went over a number of things and wanted to see if she would breast feed. She latched on like she had been doing it for weeks. They were shocked that as small as she was, five pounds, she had major can-do attitude. The next day we took her home and I don't think I stopped smiling for weeks.

Now that my daughter Madison was born, I wanted to make sure I was right on every level of my being. I had come along way, but I wanted to be perfect for her. A child changes your life.

I know what it is like to have praying parents and grandparents. I know what it is like to have your parents constantly speaking life into you, praying goodness and blessings over your life, sowing seeds for your life through tithes and offerings. They helped me to follow the principles of God and instilled them in me to counter the misguided information I was receiving from the outside world and wayward spiritual leaders and Sunday school teachers that were doing their superficial jobs without any real understanding or revelation in their own lives.

I knew that if you trained up a child in the way that they should go, then they would not part from it. No matter what I did or where I went, the Holy Spirit would bring God's word back into my remembrance, and I knew it was not my doing that protected me in the past. It was the prayers and blessings of my parents and grandparents.

I always left the door open for God, even if I did not invite Him all the way in. When I went to that door, I would receive blessings from His overflow. He still kept watch over my door and met me there when I called out to Him. He was waiting for me to get a clue, but He never left me. He waited for me. Not because I was so great, but because He had a plan for me. Because the prayers of those that came before me had already lifted prayers up on my behalf; because of their righteousness, He answered their prayers. Their prayers and righteousness kept me protected and blessed all the days of my life despite me.

I wanted to be that for Madison. And now that I felt as if I could truly trust God and understood Him, I decided to walk that path and invite Him all the way in. I put it all on the line. I no longer had the spirit of fear, but of power, and I was going to take it all the way.

On top of that, I felt God heard my cry for a child when Madison was born. I was acceptable, I thought, because He gave me my miracle child after the miscarriages, a stillbirth, and an ectopic pregnancy. Here I was after so much for so long with a beautiful baby girl. I felt God finally saw me and loved me. The truth is, He always loved me, and He always saw me—I just did not get it.

I remember praying Hannah's prayer that if He gave me a child, I would give that child back to Him all the days of its life. I finally had the only thing I really wanted and begged God for continuously, like Hannah. I searched His Word for the answer to my problem. I prayed and believed—and it worked. He gave Madison to me, *so why not give myself in return*, I thought. I could not give her in his service right now, like Hannah I would wait until she was older, but I could give myself; and when she was older, I would teach her the way to fulfill the promise and give herself to God.

I was basically saying, "God, now that I am satisfied with my life, my marriage, and my child, okay, God, now I have room for you. I will do it your way, for her sake."

My miracle child—the only thing for which I really cared enough to beg God—was here and now I was ready to build God an altar. How horrible that I was arrogant enough to say, "God, You're worthy now." But in essence, I did. Most of us do—*now that nothing else is working, I will try you, God. Now that I am alone, I will try you, God. Now that I don't know what else to do, now that I have everything I need, now that you answered this prayer or let me get away with that, I will uphold my promise and do for you now."*

People do it all the time without realizing how insulting that is. I don't think most people even recognize that is exactly what they are doing. Waiting for signs and wonders before believing and submitting. Really think about that.

Think about your child saying that to you. But just like a parent, He forgives us and overlooks the foolishness and the comment, because He is just glad that we finally get that He has our answer, and if we obey and do according to His will, things will turn out for our good. I humbled myself before Him, worshipped Him, and said, "Now, Lord, your will be done," and then, all hell broke loose.

I knew that when we take that final step the enemy will pull out every stop to hinder us from making the mark because he knows the blessing waiting on us. What I did not know and soon learned was that often the reason for which we build an altar to God is the very thing God will use to transform us. And then sometimes, the lamb to be sacrificed just might be *us*. In my case, I was the lamb tethered to that altar I built, but I was not alone—my child was inextricably bound to that altar of sacrifice along with me. Why? Because it was important to God to move me into a place of understanding and relationship with Him for the purpose for which He created me.

In our attempts to prepare to be in relationship with God, we must remember that God must be able to mold us and make us what *He* needs and wants. After all, God has had a blueprint for our lives since before the dawn of time and before the foundations of the earth (Jeremiah 1). He knows what He wants and needs.

And so here we were, my daughter and I, tied down to that altar, my child in my arms. My bottom-line issue that contributed to all of my other branching issues prior to this was fear. Fear of hurting and not being able to come back from the hurt. Fear of being a disappointment and being disappointed. Fear of succeeding, and more being expected of me. Fear of not being great. Fear of being great. Fear of being regular. Fear of not liking who I was. Fear of not liking what God would do with me. Fear of the unknown and fear of the known.

Just plain, stupid fear that played itself out in overconfidence, shyness, outspokenness, being egotistical, overcompensating, under compensating, and whatever other dysfunctional personality traits my emotions latched onto in order to aid me in expressing my frustration at not knowing who I was or wanted to be, and even more … what God wanted from me.

And now that I finally conquered fear and chose to walk in faith, I got slapped with one of the scariest times of my life. When it came to pass, I repeated to myself over and over, "I cannot go back to fear. I am free; this cannot be happening now. Is this really happening now?" I knew the enemy's trick, and he was determined to get me back in fear. I could not go back. I kept telling myself, "Don't go back, don't go backwards."

Madison was such a perfect child. She was beautiful, sweet, smart, loving. I was so in love with her. She was always with me no matter where I went. I literally did everything with her, cooking, cleaning, eating, and sleeping. You name it, I did it with her. I carried her no matter what I did. She became my arm and I was her leg.

About five months old she began throwing up and not eating much food. The doctors' response was always, "It is no big deal." I would take her to the doctor and every doctor would echo the last, she is fine, it is usual, she was born early, it is one of those things, but I could not shake it.

When Madison was six months old, I changed her diaper and noticed her stomach was uneven. I touched her stomach, and it was hard on one side. It looked like an organ had shifted out of place and was pushing out the side of her little belly. We went to the emergency room. We had been to the emergency room twice in the last few weeks because her temperature was so high. They would give her Tylenol and Motrin, get the fever under control, and send us on our way. They too responded that there was nothing wrong. "Everything is fine. This is common." Now we were once again going to the emergency room with one side of her belly protruding. *What is going on?* I wondered.

This time when we went to the emergency room they kept us waiting a long time. I still held to the belief that it was not a big deal, a surgery maybe, but she would be all right.

When all the interns started coming in to see her, Chris knew something was not right. We were both upset that no one was telling us anything, but they felt fine to tell the rest of the hospital staff to go over and touch the baby with the protruding belly as if she was the recent specimen shipped in for the class to see.

I still don't like teaching hospitals now for that reason alone. It was as if they did not understand that it was disrespectful and hurtful that they all knew what was going on, but they could not tell us. "But, oh, by the way, let me touch your baby to confirm what I know and get hands-on experience for what I can't tell you about."

I tried to stay positive, but it was obvious there was more going on behind the scenes and it could not be good. Chris was agitated, I tried to stay hopeful but was not happy with the situation either. Madison was playing as if nothing were wrong. I believed that she was fine. *Why would not she be fine? She looks fine, she acts fine.* When the last intern came in, we told them, "Look, no one else needs to come in here to touch her. We want answers, and we want to see someone who has them."

The doctors came in and still did not tell us anything specific. They just told us that she would need to stay overnight for observation. We were frustrated, and nothing made sense. Once we were checked into the hospital room, the team of specialists came in and told us the real deal. It turned out that while in the emergency room, the doctors were waiting on a specialist to come and confirm what they already knew. They were also setting up surgery and the works.

They told us that Madison had a tumor on her kidney, and they had to remove it immediately because it was huge. Chris and I looked at each other. I asked them for clarification—a tumor, but not a cancer tumor, right?

They replied emphatically, "Oh, it is cancer. We don't know what kind exactly, but we think it is Wilms' Tumor."

I could not believe this. She was six months old. I never knew of any babies having cancerous tumors at six months old. How could this be? How could this happen? This did not make sense.

Chris broke down crying. This was the fourth person in his life with cancer, and none of them ended well—his grandfather, grandmother, and mother. Now his baby had cancer. This was the worst news we could have ever gotten. I was in shock. I just kept playing it over and over in my head. *Did they just say cancer? Did they really just say cancer? Maybe cancer is a general term and covers more things than what I know. They could not have said my six-month-old miracle has cancer.*

I wished so badly for the power to turn back the hands of time. I wanted to be able to remove those words from the air, as if removing them would stop the realities of her condition. That if it were not said, it would make the tumor go away.

When Madison came down with a fever, Chris and I thought it was a typical childhood illness. No one could have imagined that a fever meant a rare form of kidney cancer. Not in my miracle! This just could not be. How could God allow this to happen? After all we had been through: miscarriages, surgeries, tubal pregnancies, a stillbirth—and now my miracle had cancer.

I thought, *why does God hate me so much?* I tried to be good and even make up for my faults, but His hand stayed against me and I could not understand. Why? Why not just punish *me*? I was not perfect and I accepted that, but she was so perfect. She was my perfect gift.

How could He give and then threaten to take away again after He had taken away so many times before? This was against Who He says He is. I gave my life to Him in complete submission because I finally believed with all of my heart that He was a good God, a loving God, slow to anger, and He desired my peace, prosperity, and wellness. But now I could not understand who He was and why He would not protect me; instead, He hated me.

Why me? Why again? I loved her. I would die for her. I would die with her. So many people don't love their children. They don't care that they have children, and yet they have no issues. I tried to do everything right, and still I was losing. I clutched her tightly to me. I laid my head against her body, and though I was in shock, trying to catch my breath, and not in an active cry, the tears rolled like waterfalls.

I felt the piercing, hot sharp pangs of the doctor's words, like razor-sharp knives maliciously stabbing me in my heart over and over again—ripping me apart from my throat to my belly. Every word was a vengeful thrust and an excruciating upper cut.

I could not cry at first for some reason. I now understand what people mean when they say, "It was like the air was sucked out of the room." It *was* like all the air was sucked out of the room, and I was hoping all the air was gone and

I would die right there. Somewhere from deep inside me, a moan rattled up and out.

My soul shrilled in contempt of what I was hearing. A familiar sound I'd never uttered before, but had heard long ago in one of my grandmother's crying episodes over the loss of my grandfather. And I'd heard such moans twice before from my father—upon the death of my grandmother and my Uncle Edgar, his brother. A moan that defies description because it is uttered by the human spirit, and only God and the Holy Spirit understand it and can respond to it.

Romans 8:26–28 speaks of the Holy Spirit standing in the gap for us. *The Spirit helps us in our weakness. We do not know what we ought to pray for, but the Spirit himself intercedes for us with groans that words cannot express. And he who searches our hearts knows the mind of the Spirit, because the Spirit intercedes for the saints in accordance with God's will.*

I was hoping the Holy Spirit was interceding for me at that time, because if I had spoken to God out of my despair and anger, it would have turned into more of a hate speech than prayer, and I did not want that.

I knew better than that now. I was redeemed. I truly believed. I walked by faith and not by sight. I believed I was the fullness of all God created me to be. But now I felt like I was a shell who had no voice, who felt powerless, who wanted to die. I was in a contradiction. It hurt too much.

What I felt and what I knew did not mesh and what I was hearing did not compute. I was in a strange land. I felt like I had left my body and entered someone else's life. This was not me. This was not my life. This was not my child's diagnosis.

Chris and I were both so hurt. Chris did not ever want to have another child. He was tired, too. Tired of being hurt and disappointed. We cried together, and all we could think about was *why*. What were we doing so wrong that God would allow this to happen to us over and over?

As soon as I gave in to the tears, I felt the release of my strength. As if I were a diver doing a two-and-a-half back flip somersault, headed for the water in slow-mo, I felt myself falling into resignation. I wanted to give up on everything. I was so tired and so outdone. But … I was afraid that if I gave in, it would be the end; and so, I needed to fight. Despite what I felt, I knew what I was supposed to do.

My anger and frustration were transformed into focus. I just had to figure out what was going on. *What was this all about?* There was more to this than I knew, and I had to get focused. This was the enemy, not God. But God would use this for my good. I knew He was in this; He knew my trouble.

Chris and I needed a fight plan, and we needed to focus on winning. The enemy wanted us to give up, he wanted me to fear, but I could not let him win. I was not losing to him anymore. I was sick of him. I had to figure this thing out, I told myself.

We soon managed to pull ourselves together and took heart: *she has cancer, but she is still here.*

## Chapter Six

# The Valley of Shadows

*The steps of a good man are ordered by the Lord, and He delights in his way. Though he fall, he shall not be utterly cast down; For the Lord upholds him with His hand.*
*(Psalm 37:23–24)*

I HAD BEEN BEFORE THE Lord for months prior to this, developing a relationship of truth and power. I believed that this was just the devil trying to push me back into my safety zone or drag out the spirit of fear I had packed away. Trying to convince me that following God meant untold suffering. Well, I knew that before I surrendered and embarked on this path.

*Then Peter began to say to Him, "See, we have left all and followed You." So Jesus answered and said, "Assuredly, I say to you, there is no one who has left house or brothers or sisters or father or mother or wife or children or lands, for My sake and the gospel's, who shall not receive a hundredfold now in this time—houses and brothers and sisters and mothers and children and lands, with persecutions—and in the age to come, eternal life* (Mark 10:28–30).

I knew that persecution came with the territory, not because God brings persecution, but because the enemy brings it against us through people (haters, liars, thieves, jealousy, envy), through strife, disease, loss and so on. The enemy only knows what God allows him to know and sometimes we forget that. But what he knows is still enough for him to *try* and get in the way. It is vitally important to get into the will of God and start operating in His principles and anointing and overflow. The enemy tries to destroy our faith in God, hoping to stop the flow of everything God is doing and in turn, stop us from being blessed and being a blessing to others.

The enemy comes to contradict and steal the Word from our hearts so that the Word will not grow and bring forth fruit in our lives. He comes to accuse God, accuse His Word, and bring condemnation of our past sins. BUT…

*There is therefore now no condemnation to those who are in Christ Jesus, who do not walk according to the flesh, but according to the Spirit.* (Romans 8:1)

He tries to get us to question God. If he impairs or destroys our faith, he gets our future. Trials, tribulations and persecution are the enemy's way to cause confusion and doubt in the Word and the ability of God. God uses these situations to show Himself strong on our behalf when He heals, rescues and delivers us from evil.

But I already knew the Word and believed and received God and His Word. The enemy was dealing with the new me. I was good soil and the seed of God's Word was planted and secure. So now the enemy wanted to stop my harvest. If he can't get the seed, he will go after the harvest.

I was aware of his ways and that was why I stayed in my safe zone so long before this. But I was wiser now. I knew that safe zones only kept me in fear and bondage and did not keep me from anything. I knew that the reason the devil did not mess with me in my safe zone is because in that state

I was disengaged from my source and I was not operating under the full power and authority of God. Therefore, I was no threat to the devil or his kingdom. I actually enable him by *not* doing what I have been called to do. My life brings nothing to the table without the God that created and purposed my existence.

God knows why I was created, where I am to go, and what I am to do. When we are connected to our Creator, we operate at full potential, successfully (Joshua 1:8). However, on our own – so to speak – we have no revealed purpose and no visible or conscious greatness.

Although the power is on in our homes, until we flip the switch, there is no connection to the source and consequently, no light, no direct power to run dishwashers, vacuums, blow dryers and the such.

The devil attempts to destroy the witness of God's people and tries to scare us into retreat. The enemy hopes we will turn from God and doubt the truth. The enemy tempts us, hoping we will stumble.

*But he who received the seed on stony places, this is he who hears the word and immediately receives it with joy; yet he has no root in himself, but endures only for a while. For when tribulation or persecution arises because of the word, immediately he stumbles.* (Matthew 13:20–21)

I knew that because of the revelation given to me of who I am in Christ Jesus, my confidence in that truth was being tested. I needed to be good soil and not stony soil. I could not allow the enemy to bring something against me that would cause me to doubt the truth. I knew that my persecutions and tribulations did not change the Word, but the Word would change me and the outcome of what had come against me. The Word would cause those tribulations to work out for my good or to be moved completely out of my way.

I got clear on the fact that if I remained steadfast and faithful and fulfilled my purpose in this situation, I would be rewarded and my prayers would be answered. I knew that others would be blessed by the victory. God would win more souls and bless and rescue more people from what bound them in their minds and spirits, because I was no longer blind to my purpose and lived in the abundance of who God created me to be.

*Immediately there fell from his eyes something like scales, and he received his sight at once; and he arose and was baptized* (Acts 9:18).

Chris and I were determined that we were not going to let the enemy win this. Not spiritually and not physically. Cancer was not to be the victor. We knew it was going to be a battle, but we were convinced that we would have the victory. So we went in search of what God was saying in the midst of this. What was His purpose, and what were we to get out of this? What were we to learn from this, and how did it play in God's ultimate plan for us?

We prayed, we fasted, and we believed. For a long while, it seemed all was well. On top of that, her diagnosis was 90 percent curable. She had no side effects or issues with the chemotherapy, and she did not lose her hair. She had no problems growing; though she did not gain a lot of weight, she was in perfect health except for the tumor. We proclaimed victory every day.

Three months after Madison's initial diagnosis, right before the end of her chemotherapy treatments, she began having problems breathing.

We took her to her oncologist, who sent us for X-rays to see if there was something going on with her lungs. Often, those undergoing chemotherapy can have complications that will cause fluid to build in the lungs.

X-rays had been taken of her chest just seven days prior to this, and all was well. So I did not think much of it. I thought there may be some fluid in her lungs, they would have to put in chest tubes to get it out, and we would move on. The chemo regimen was scheduled to end in another month. I thought to myself, *we will deal with this and move on. It is almost over.*

Here we were going in for another X-ray to see if there was fluid in her lungs, and instead we found that the cancer had spread throughout her body while she was on chemo. This happened in seven days. No one understood why or how.

They definitely could not explain how in seven days she went from zero cancer to being full of cancer in her abdomen and chest. Seven days prior, a week before, she had all of these scans, X-rays, and other checkups, and had no sign of cancer or anything else. Now, only one week later, she had three large tumors in her chest alone around her heart and lungs, and where they took her kidney out was a tumor in place of the kidney.

No one had an answer. The doctors from Virginia contacted other hospitals and specialists around the country to see if anyone else had experienced this and to get a consensus on diagnosis and treatment.    A l m o s t everyone said there had to be something wrong with the diagnosis. They had the samples tested three times in three different places, and they all came back with the same result; however, the diagnosis and the action of the cancer were not consistent.

They concluded that she had to have been misdiagnosed and that she actually had the rarest of the rarest forms of kidney cancer, Rhabdoid Wilms. The cancer is so rare that out of a half billion people in North America, less than a hundred, all children, are diagnosed with this type of cancer each year.

They decided to treat her for Rhabdoid Wilms instead of the regular Wilms tumor. They were not absolutely sure if it was Rhabdoid or just plain Wilms, but no matter what kind of cancer she had, the chemo regimen for Rhabdoid was the most potent; if it did not work on whatever she had, they did not have anything else. Out of millions, less than a hundred children—and my baby was a part of this unlucky number. How could this be?

If I thought chemo, radiation, doctors, treatments, healthy eating, or anything else was the cure for what I was against, I was definitely proven wrong. Everyone was wrong and confused. Nothing worked, and nothing made sense. Whether the doctors wanted to admit it or not, they did not have a clue. That is why it is called *practicing* medicine. God complexes they may have, but God they are not.

No one can read a book written by another man and become God. All of my hope was in God. I could not hope that things in the natural world would work in conjunction with the grace and leading of God; it was God or nothing.

I soon learned that none of the doctors I regularly dealt with on the medical team believed in God. For a short time, I was a little perturbed by them for not believing with me and for me. It bothered me that they had no hope.

I did not think the doctors had to be religious but I did want them to have hope. I wanted them to believe in something, the possibility of good, to be positive and look and think outside the box. If you always follow a recipe you will always get the same result, but if you try something different, you can get something different.

Knowing that God can do all things, I believed that God could and would work for their good as well. I knew I had to stay in love to stay in the right spirit to be open to God, His voice, His leading. But during the ordeal, I had pity on the doctors when I knew they secretly pitied me. I had compassion for them, for the peace they were missing.

As doctors, they have seen not only what I went through, but others losing children to horrible diseases and sometimes very minor issues that should be curable. They deal with this over and over again. I can see how not having an understanding of God and spiritual things leads to doubt and even the denial of the existence of God. And trust is placed in statistics and medicine. After all, to the natural eye, that seems to be more reliable.

Think about it: how can a loving God allow such suffering, denying the hopes and prayers of those who are suffering, especially innocent children? I better understood later, and I forgave them and forgave myself for how I felt at the time.

The nurses, on the other hand, were truly a blessing. Many prayed with or for my family often. They were very attentive and kind. A lot of the specialists that I dealt with were also just as wonderful. The other doctors' lack of spiritual understanding, evasiveness and lack of belief in anything other than themselves did not comfort me. However, it caused me to really stay close to the throne of God. He was all I had.

When the doctors checked Madison into the hospital after the cancer spread, they set up emergency radiation treatments. The Spirit told me to pray.

I shrugged it off and said, "No, I will pray when we get there. I will pray over her in the room."

It was taking a long time for them to get things set up, and we kept getting delayed. I heard the Spirit say, "No, pray now."

So while they were prepping her and we were waiting for word on a possible transport time, I prayed. As soon as I said, "Amen," the nurse came in and said, "We can actually go right now, let's go."

On the way down to radiation, there were a lot of people everywhere in the hospital halls. As we made our way through the halls, I prayed. I prayed the whole way down to the radiation department. We turned down a hall toward the radiation treatment area.

This hall was not full of people as the other halls were. Out of nowhere, a man appeared behind me. He walked up on me and my husband really fast. I could feel him almost immediately walking lockstep with one of the nurses behind us, but I did not turn around.

When I heard the sound of ice rattling in a cup, I turned around. As I turned to my right to face the man, he moved to my left rear. I turned to my left, and I only caught a glimpse of his face and shirt at the edge of my vision. He appeared to be a fifteen- to eighteen-year-old Caucasian male. He was dressed sort of like a skateboarder, but there was nothing unusual about him until he spoke.

From the left behind me, he said, "May God be with you."

"Thank you," I said and looked at my husband Chris. Chris had heard him, too, and also replied. But when we turned, he was not there. Neither was the sound of his walking and rattling ice. The nurse that was behind us turned down the intersecting hall alone.

After the radiation treatment, as we were on our way back to the room, a middle-aged African American woman was standing alone in the hall, leaning against the wall bundled up in a hat, scarf, and winter coat. She was speaking on her cell phone. Chris and I passed her and suddenly both turned back toward her direction. I can't explain what exactly made us turn around, but we did.

We realized she was not talking on the phone, but was speaking to us. She repeated what we'd missed: "God is with you, believe in God." We both thanked her.

"I am praying for you," she said.

I believe even to this day that God sends his angels but we are not always paying attention. There are no coincidences. How often have any of us entertained angels in disguise? After all, they are sent to minister for God's people (Hebrews 1:14).

I was in the hospital for weeks. I prayed and fasted and prayed and read the Word over and over every day. I read the Word and prayed over Madison and into my own spirit daily for hours. I confessed the promises of the Word over her and never left her alone in the hospital.

The doctors were confused when Madison was doing well. And amazed again when she did not do well. They could not explain why she was not progressing or responding to treatments. What I had was prayer and my faith in God that no matter what, He was still in control and would see that everything worked out for the good of all—not just myself.

A few weeks later, they told us she would not make it and to prepare for her death. They took us into a room with all of the doctors, the specialists, the chaplains, and tissues. When they told us this, they all sat still waiting for the drama and despair. Chris did not say a word.

I smiled at them all and said, "I know you think we are going to break down. I see you have come prepared with your tissues and grief staff, but that is not what is going to happen here. You do what you can, and God will do the rest. I have not given up, and until she is gone, she is meant to be here. We are all right, don't worry about us; you just do what you are supposed to, and everything will work out fine."

Some of them were doing that eye thing that people do. You know, the one where you shoot a glance across the room that states, "Are they crazy? Did I just hear what I thought I heard? Is this for real? They are going to be in for a rude awakening. Okay, you don't have to believe us, be in denial." The rest just continued looking at us.

One specialist that we had dealt with before, who did Madison's first surgery to remove her kidney, spoke in his beautiful calm spirit with a look of compassion, concern, and hope. He was one of the few doctors that showed real compassion, but I'd only dealt with him twice. He said something very nice, and we said, "Okay. You all have a nice day."

Everyone else slowly got up from their seats, looking around waiting for more. It was obvious the residents were told to be prepared for the fallout, and they were truly waiting and wondering what just happened. I wanted to say, "Faith happened, and no one in this room has the last word. When He tells me to let go, I will. Until then, I will continue to hold on for the promises of His Word to manifest on the earth, in my baby's body."

They had her in an induced coma doing regular intense chemotherapy and radiation therapy. Her body refused to absorb the fluid in its tissue, and her body blew up three times its size. The chest tubes they put in were taped to her back and sides. When she swelled up, the tape pulled her skin off of her body. It was one thing after another. But I kept speaking life over her. I prayed and fasted every day, proclaiming her healing. "By your stripes she is healed, no weapon formed against her will prosper, we are more than conquerors, this too shall pass, she is healed, the devil is a liar, and let every word of the Lord be true."

I prayed every three hours and read the Word over her and spoke to her every few hours. I got to know most of the nurses and fell in love with them. They became my family, and I would help them do things with Madison and for her. Change the bedding, clean things, roll her and reposition her just so I could touch her and hold her. I felt so empty without her calling me or needing me. I needed her to be all right.

Everything I needed at that moment was connected to machines, and nobody trusted her ability to be all right. I fought for her with everything I had in me. I never knew love like that. I never cared like that. I had never been desperate like that.

After about fourteen or fifteen days in the hospital, I had a dream that all of the machines were taken off Madison. She sat up in the bed, back to her regular size, and a spider came up out of her mouth. She then drank from a bottle. Something she had never done; she was a breast-fed baby.

The next day Madison got better, and the doctors had no explanation for it. All of a sudden while I was talking to a nurse, Madison's body just started shrinking back to size, her kidneys started working, and the catheter was filled with urine. Things changed instantly.

I rejoiced and confessed what I knew: God did it. Within days of the incident in the room with the medical staff, Madison was off all of the machines and doing well—out of the induced coma, off of the ventilator, breathing on her own, no problems whatsoever, and the first thing she did was drink from a bottle. Twenty-one days in the hospital in ICU, and we were now leaving.

The cancer was still present in her body, but she was fine. They were astonished—how could this be? How was she breathing and eating and living when no medical intervention was working? The tumors were still present, still the same size, but they were not causing her any issues. I knew it was God. Within a week after leaving the hospital, she was back to herself. I just knew that God had performed a miracle and Madison was healed.

I believed it was finished. God dealt with me greatly in the hospital. Sometimes God has to get you in a place where you have no other choice but to look up. In my seeking a healing for Madison, I received a healing and transformation of my soul, mind, and spirit.

I read the Word and meditated on it constantly. God would speak so clearly. Every day, all day, more revelation. It was amazing. I did not know I had it in me. I did not. God formed it in me and then drew it out. I did not know I could have that kind of relationship with the Father.

I would pray and meditate and ask God a question. When I moved, the pages of the Bible would turn. I would look down to the page, and there was the answer to my question. I would pray about something, and the Spirit would lead me to read one of the three spiritual texts I took with me to the hospital—and there was the answer. Things became so much clearer. I could hear God speak in a still, quiet voice. The voice that you know is not you because you could not tell yourself the things that are imparted to you.

I began to crave God's Word, His voice, and His way, not just for Madison's healing, but for my relationship with God. I fell in love with God, with myself, with humanity, with existence. I found love and desired to abide in that love with God. I wanted it to consume me. I knew, with the way

God dealt with me in the hospital day after day, that He was not just transforming me, but He had transformed my baby's condition. She was healed.

I knew that God had said yes, not only because she was doing well, but because He'd healed my mind and spirit. It just made sense. He'd breathed truth into my spirit. He'd poured His Spirit and mind into me, and faith was restored. He had imprinted Himself on me. The door was open to fellowship with Him. I realized that through Christ I had the power to call things that were not as though they were and they would come to pass. I could speak to the mountain, and it had to move. I had faith not only in God, but the power of God that lives in me.

I realized that everything I wanted, I already possessed, and that was also the same for Madison. The healing I wanted for her was already hers; it was already mine. This was the beginning of new life and new understanding.

Madison's ordeal was used to change me and my husband. God used her to do more for us than we could do for her. We began telling all of our family and friends what God had done. We told them about our experience. We shared how God would speak so clearly to us through dreams, visions, His Word and how the dreams we had would come to pass. God was with us every step of the way. It was an amazing journey. I just knew He could not take me on a journey like this and not bring me all the way through. He had to see this thing through. I believed that it was written as such.

I knew that I had never been without God, even through the dark times. He was always there comforting me, preparing me, and strengthening me through His Word and through others. It was an amazing experience. I knew I was changed forever. I had been to a point of no return. I trusted God that things would not just work out for the good of Chris and myself, but that Madison's healing and her life on earth was for our good, not her death - but her life.

It would be an encouragement and testimony for the good of those around us watching and praying with us. I felt I finally had the relationship and understanding with God that I'd always wanted.

Fear and confusion were gone forever; I was walking in His power. His power was mighty, and I sincerely believed that I now knew the mode of operation of God. I walked in confidence of who He was and who I was in Him.

I woke up one night after all of this to see a line of light traveling through the house. Sleep was on me so hard, I did not have the strength to get up and follow it. The same night, Chris had a dream that he was in the room, but the entire room was lit up. He then began walking along a road toward two stars holding Madison's hand as she walked beside him toward the stars. As he was walking along, going higher and higher, further and further on a road, he became aware of God's presence in the light before him.

Chris asked, "God, is that you?"

The voice said, "Yes, I am God. I am with you."

Knowing that God was with us, that God had been with us, and that He showed Himself throughout this ordeal, we believed that this season was over and our prayers were answered as we desired.

All of our dreams and visions of God told us that everything would be all right. When I would pray, I could hear the Holy Spirit say that everything was going to be all right. God is with us.

The last week of May I saw death. I had seen it before, but knowing that God was telling me I would be all right, that Madison would be all right, I thought my binding and rebuking was the end of it. That week I went to the doctor because I discovered I was pregnant and having some issues. An ultrasound was ordered. During the exam, the technician was unable to find the baby. She looked further and discovered the baby was stuck in the fallopian tube. Here I was in the midst of one of the worst fights of my life with an ectopic pregnancy.

Upon further examination by the specialist, we were told that my tube was about to explode and had begun filling with fluid. He could not believe I had no pain. They told me that if I had waited any longer, I would have died from the contamination in my body from the eruption of the tube.

The baby had to be removed immediately in order to save my life. I had to have surgery that same day. I thought this was what the death vision was about. Before this, I prayed that God would take me in Madison's place. I wanted God to give her a chance at life. But recently I had changed that prayer and was now asking to stay with her so she would not have to deal with all of the aftermath of her cancer and the side effects of her surgeries and treatments without a mother.

I wanted her to stay with me, and I wanted to be with her. I felt that maybe God had answered that prayer and interceded on my behalf.

I thought maybe, once again, He'd told death *no* and that was why I was able to make it to the doctor before my own death. However, that still meant that death was taking my unborn child. It was hurtful and confusing, and more questions were added to my test. I was losing one child while trying to hold on to another.

I wanted to know if this was it. Was there more to this nightmare? How much more? But I was scared to ask. I was afraid to ask anymore from God. I was scared of what He would show me. I was afraid there would be more and that more would be too much to handle.

I wanted so badly to step back and live in a delusion for a minute. I wanted to have faith in my own truth, because for the moment, God's truth was too much to bear; there was still too much to hold out for and hold on to. I needed it to be over and that I had nothing else to pray about or hope for. That I did not have to keep PUSH-ing (pray until something happens).

I needed to believe my tomorrow was present, not in the spirit, but in the natural. I wanted my joy to come the very next morning, because any more days in battle would kill me. But I had come too far. I had to finish the race. I could not give up now, though the pressure was mounting.

The next day Madison had to go back to the hospital. It was not over. What was worse was that I could not go with her to the hospital. All this time I had always been with her, praying, hoping, believing, loving, and reassuring us both it would be all right. I prayed and stood strong in the Word, keeping death far away, but not this time. I had surgery the night before, so Chris went with her and stayed with her at the hospital.

The day before she came home, death was at the door again. I tried to fight it this time with all of my might as well as with my words. I spoke everything I could against it. I screamed and pleaded with God because I knew death was not here on its own this time. When I would speak against it before, it would always go away. This time it loomed at the door. It had a mission that had a specific time, and it could hesitate no more. While rebuking it and commanding it kept it from coming closer, it did not leave the door. Since I knew it was there by a higher authority, I pleaded to its Commander, God Himself. I began to walk to the door screaming, crying, and mad at death for not leaving this time, praying to God to change its course.

I fell through the door where death was standing and found myself standing in Madison's hospital room. She was so beautiful and looked like her old self. She was perfectly healed. I kept saying to myself – "she is perfect, she is perfectly healed," encouraging myself, believing the good I saw, the beauty I saw. Trying to call what I saw in the spirit to be in the natural.

She had on all white silk, and her bed was all white silk with ruffles. The room was bright with white light, and Chris was lying in the bed next to her. Madison woke up and looked at me with her big eyes and long eyelashes, and she spoke something that I could not make out. I walked closer to her bed to make out what she was saying to me. She looked like a doll, she was so beautiful.

Chris woke up when she spoke and asked what I was doing there and how I got to the hospital. I told him I had to come see her - that God brought me to see that she was all right.

Look at her. She has perfect healing. She is so beautiful. I kept saying she was all right, everything was all right. In my head I was thinking that meant she was going to live. That she would live the life I desired for her - that what I saw was right now, not in spirit, but in the earth. That her being healed meant no more doctors, hospitals, or issues with cancer or treatments.

I was riding high in my confidence that everything was going to be all right, God was with us. That had to mean that what I believed in faith was to manifest on the earth.

The chemo regimen was more extreme and we were in the hospital every so many weeks for days at a time for chemo and evaluations. Madison began to lose her hair, her skin darkened and she did not gain much weight. Despite all of this she was happy, wonderfully pleasant and content.

We threw a huge birthday bash for her with over two hundred people. We had jump houses, clowns, snow cone machine, cotton candy makers, catered barbeque, custom balloon towers, ornaments and a ton of other stuff. We went all out. The theme was *Celebration of Life* and we did just that.

It was so much fun. The next few weekends we went to the mall, hung out, ate out, did all the normal stuff. We celebrated Mother's Day and felt like a normal family again. We felt like we were on the road to recovery. We went and got Madison her first real pair of shoes from Stride-Rite and took pictures with her shoes on. When we got home Chris and Madison both fell asleep while we watched a movie. That night Madison slept the best she had in a while sprawled out across Chris as if he were the mattress. I took a picture of them sleeping. It made me feel so happy. I felt like I had my family back.

The next day Madison's fever was sky high again. We went to the emergency room. She had an infection. I was relieved. But for the next few weeks we were in and out of the emergency room and the hospital for chemo or some new side effect.

Then Madison's body appeared to shut down from everything that was going on. She developed ascities and her belly filled up with fluid and she stopped urinating. They told us there was not anything they could do. I still believed God would work a miracle for me. I was told this same thing before and she came out fine, she is still here.

Knowing that God does heal made me hold on. I kept the faith. Until He says it is over I was holding on. *If He saved her before, He could save her again and this time, take the cancer away,* I thought to myself. Even though to the natural eye it seemed it was not purposed for me, I knew He could do it, so I continued to press toward that. I refused to *not* have faith and, instead, believed in His healing power.

I operated in the spirit of *yes*. God gave Hezekiah fifteen extra years when he prayed against his death. He gave my great grandmother many years after her abdominal cancer ate through her body so badly she had to be tied to a chair just to hold her body up. The doctors sent her home to die and she was eventually confined to a bed, only for God to heal her and all the cancer in her body disappear. She never had a problem again and walked, ate, and did whatever until her death late into her nineties.

My father is still alive after the doctors told us he only had days to live when his organs shut down and his fever was so high his skin began to boil. One day while they were waiting to give him his last rites in the ICU, an angel came to my father in his coma and told my father he would be healed. While he was walking with that angel in spirit, my mother, sitting in the room next to my father's bed, saw a hand that appeared in the room in a surgical glove, and it started taking the machine wires off of my father.

A voice told her it was going to be all right. The voice that spoke told her to tell that if anyone asked about the hand, "Tell them it was the hand of A Man." My dad was restored that day and, sure enough, the medical team came in and removed everything that hand had touched.

God gave Madison more time after they told us she was not going to make it out of the hospital, and she instantly turned around. He could give her more time again. He could do it. He can delay. I will hold on. Too many before me have been at death's door only for it to be closed and life breathed back into them. That too, is for me. I will trust it.

On the twelfth of June, Madison died from an infection in her stomach that caused cardiac arrest. BAM! Back to square one. I did not understand. I felt lost again. Just when it all made sense, suddenly, it did not. I was in the dark again. I felt like Gideon—this could not be my promise. What was happening? Why was God not the God of my ancestors? Why did He not hear my call and answer? Why did the promises of His Word not manifest in my situation as I trusted they would?

*And the Angel of the Lord appeared to him, and said to him, "The Lord is with you, you mighty man of valor!" Gideon said to Him, "O my lord if the Lord is with us, why then has all this happened to us? And where are all His miracles which our fathers told us about, saying, 'Did not the Lord bring us up from Egypt?' But now the Lord has forsaken us and delivered us into the hands of the Midiantes"* (Judg. 6:12–13).

I thought, *Not another curve, Lord. I can't take this ride; please kill me now!*

I could not take anymore. The day she passed, she was very quiet and only wanted to be held. She seemed so weak, but so bright and beautiful. Her eyes had peace in them, but there was a distance, even though her actions showed she wanted to remain close and be held.

Whenever I would put her down, it seemed to take so much for her to hold her arms up to be held again. She would put her arms out, and her eyes would beg to be held. She did not say anything verbally; only her eyes spoke. Every time I went to the kitchen, I would turn to look at her and her arms would be outstretched to me. I would go to her and talk to her and kiss her, and she only looked at me.

I think deep down I knew what was happening, but I also knew God was the Healer. I just knew He could and would answer my prayer. Even at the eleventh hour. She did not have to go. He would heal her. Her healing would manifest any moment now. I knew it could change in an instant just like it did in the hospital. A miracle was coming. It was mine. I continued having visions and at the end of them everything would always be okay. I was convinced He would do it, but she was suddenly so weak.

I begged Him, "Lord, heal her, and do it quickly because my baby is slipping away. I call healing now! You said it would be all right. This is not all right."

Soon her breathing was labored, and it became loud. I called Chris to come home and I began to pray over her. She got better. The breathing slowed, and in her eyes I could see that she was returning to me. She opened her eyes and smiled. She spoke and reached toward my face with her hands, and I praised God. Then she went back again. This happened two more times.

There was a small glass angel hanging on a picture frame on the entertainment center with Madison's name on it. It sat in front of a row of pictures of Madison. The last time I prayed over her, that same glass angel with her name on it fell from the top of the frame and hit the shelf. *Bam!* That little angel hit the shelf as if it weighed one hundred pounds. The sound was piercing, like a bullet rang out and pierced through my body.

I screamed, "No, God, please no!!!"

I called the ambulance. By then, Chris was home. He took Madison from me. Her body was limp. I thought she was already gone, but he took her into another room and fell to the floor on his knees still holding her, crying and praying. For a moment, she was back.

We laid her on the floor as the emergency operator talked us through resuscitation. She told me to check her mouth to make sure she was not choking on anything that would cause her breathing to be labored, but her jaws had locked.

I knew what was happening, but I had to fight for my baby. I refused to accept it. Chris and I cried and prayed. He blew in her mouth as instructed, and Madison kissed him and began blowing at him. She was laughing, razzing with her mouth, talking and moving. She was doing her usual antics, but she was so delicate. We just cried and smiled through our tears, looking at our baby—waiting for something more. It did not come. Soon she was gone again, just lying there.

The ambulance finally arrived, and we were on the way to the hospital. They gave her oxygen to sustain her in the ambulance, and she cried a small faint cry off and on, annoyed by the mask, but too frail to remove it herself.

When we got to the hospital, we went into a small side room and prayed. I accepted the fact that God never said she would live, He only told me we would be all right and everything would work out.

I wanted to believe that it would work out the way *I* wanted it to work out. I wanted my desire to be a part of His will, but I had to accept that this was not about me, this was bigger than me. And if His Word is true, if He is true, I had to trust that everything would be all right. But I would not let go of the idea that my desire would be granted and that He would keep her with me. I refused to understand that it could work any other way, but I had to accept that it might. I had to, but I did not want to. I did not know how.

Chris and I prayed and told God that if it were not His will for her to be here with us any longer and she had fulfilled her purpose, then take her quickly and don't let her suffer any longer. But if it was not His will to take her away, then intercede now. I told God "I have faith she is to stay. I can't let go of her, but if she has to go, let me know for sure. Let me know to let go because I can't seem to do it and I will fight if it is Your will for her to stay, I will keep going." We left the room and went to her bed to lie with her. We just kept praying over her and stroking her.

For a while she just looked around, not saying anything. Then she reached out to Chris, trying to get out of the bed, and began crying out "Dada, Dada," in a loud and heartbreaking cry—as if she were being pulled away from us and she were trying to hold on. That's when I realized she was only staying for us. She held on for us because we could not let go. She was as connected to our love as we were to her love.

Then we prayed the prayer that finally allowed God to finish. We just said, "Lord, Your will be done. We surrender to your will." She could not leave - she could not die because God had to honor our prayer, our faith. The end result written in her book of life was still preordained, but He answers the fervent prayer of the righteous and our prayer was for her to stay and live. He gave her more time to help us come to a place where we could let her go and realize she had fought the good fight and fulfilled her purpose. She left us again. It was so hard to watch her go back and forth. It hurt so much!

I held her tight ... hoping if she felt my spirit, her spirit would stay, and God would heal her so that she could stay because we loved each other so much. I just hoped that if He knew how much she wanted to stay and be with me and how much I wanted her to stay and be with me, He would change His mind.

The whole time I did not stop having faith that a miracle was about to happen. That everything I thought and everything He showed me to let me know everything would be all right meant that at the end, she would come back around like she did before. That God would not do this to me.

God said He would not forsake me or make me ashamed. I had stood on His Word and proclaimed the good news— but her death was not good news. How would that help anyone else? How do you call me to tell the miracle that ends in death? That makes no sense. Death made no sense to me, so I waited for the miracle. If I gave it to God and His will be done, greatness was surely going to come, not death. *I will walk by faith and not by sight,* I told myself, *just give it to God. Maybe I am in the way. Maybe I should stop praying for my desire and just stick with His will be done, His will be done. What is going to move you, Lord? What will move this mountain I thought was gone?*

*He pulled away from them about a stone's throw, knelt down, and prayed, "Father, remove this cup from me. But please, not what I want. What do you want?" At once an angel from heaven was at his side, strengthening him. He prayed on all the harder. Sweat, wrung from him like drops of blood, poured off his face* (Luke 22:42–43).

Madison was becoming so cold, and her breathing was so labored.... I could not seem to get her comfortable. I could feel her body getting stiff, so I laid her on the bed.

When I laid her down, she went limp, and dark red blood came out of her nose and then her mouth. I screamed, falling to the floor, feeling so defeated and so empty.

There was a screaming from my soul:
*God, NO!!! You have forsaken me!*
*You have forsaken me again!*
*You have forsaken me!*
*I trusted you and I believed you, and you still failed me. You transformed me for what, to leave me, to disappoint me?*

*All that you healed in me means nothing because I am so confused.*

*There is no pleasing you—it is in vain.*

*You forsake those that love you and try your way!*

*You took my everything! My baby, my hope—my God—my faith and my trust.*

*It is all gone.*

*It was all in vain.*

*Why do I live for you, only to be hurt?*

Despite what I knew and I prayed, the pain was unbearable and spoke louder than my knowledge.

## Chapter Seven

# I Will Fear No Evil

*Rest in the Lord, and wait patiently for Him... Cease from anger,*
*and forsake wrath; Do not fret—it only causes harm*
*(Ps. 37:7–8).*

THEN I HEARD A SMALL voice say, *Get up.*

I said, "No, you forsook me. You cannot tell me anything anymore, I am through."

I heard the voice say again, *Get up. You know better than this, you have come too far. Shut up and get up.* But I did not.

"No, you let these disbelieving heathens win. They told me You would not do anything, and in their God-complex, they told me how they know more and do more than You, and I told them that my God is bigger than man, his science, and his arrogance. After all of that, You allowed the wicked to win again."

God said,

*I am God whether they believe or not.*

*Baby, my child, I did not forsake you.*

*My Son said the same thing.*

*But He understood it was bigger than Him and those that seemed to be victorious over Him.*

*He submitted to the path set before Him and said, "it is finished."*

*Now it is your time to say, "It is finished,"*

*and understand it is bigger than you.*
*I have taught you too much.*
*Know that it is bigger than what you see and are experiencing, and it **will** work out in the end for the better good of you and all you reach.*

I still lay there for a while. I was so defeated. So broken. So angry. I hated God, I hated life, I hated everything and everyone. I wanted Him to kill me. But death would not come for me. I wanted it to come, I wanted God to be mad enough to kill me for being mad at Him, but I knew He was right. I hated that He was right, but I had nothing else. Where was I to go, whose would I be, what am I without Him and everything I know? He called me His child, I do belong to Him. There is no escaping the truth.

If I went too far and escaped into myself, I knew I would not come back, and that would mean more pain for everyone else. So I pulled myself off the floor. It was hard—I really just wanted God to kill me. Kill me so I could be with my baby. I begged Him to let me go with her, to let me die; I did not want to do this life anymore. The only thing that made me get up other than the words I heard was the idea of Chris losing me right after losing our child. I could not do that to him. But I wanted to go.

This life was not worth it. Hopes and dreams seemed to shatter before they got off the ground.

So I said it: "It is finished. I know *better* than what I feel. But God, so much of me died with her, I have nothing left."

And I heard Him answer that, too. He said,

*"All that you wanted for her, all that you needed for her, I have given to you. You needed healing, love, strength, change, and transformation. I needed you, and she helped me to finally heal and free you.*

*"I know it hurts, but I did not bring you this far to leave you. You feel so much has died, but with death comes life. Madison's death has brought you more life and life abundantly. You will realize why she came.*

*"She is one of the many to follow in the footsteps of Jesus, bringing life through her death and transformation through her life and the overcoming of all obstacles."*

No doctor, no man, no prophet can fully explain anything that God is involved in until it is over. Though they try, the truth is that when God is involved, whether we perceive what's happening as good or bad, no one can explain it; we can only react or act in that which we are handed and wait for the full story to unfold. There is always more to the story.

From conception, no one was ever able to dictate or predict anything with Madison. We could only react with joy or sorrow. Many were called in to confer because of the unexplainable and unpredictable from her birth until her passing. God was right.

I got up off the floor saying "it is all right, I am all right, we are all right, it is finished, it is all right." I could see everyone's face looking to see if I had cracked, if I left myself on the floor. Wondering why I kept talking to myself, yelling at myself. I pulled myself solid on my feet and I went to Chris to get my baby and I held the cold empty body that once housed my beautiful baby girl. I sang to her, I kissed her, I stroked her, and I cried for her. I cried for my husband, and I cried for myself.

I hoped that God's Word would still prove true for me, because His Word was all I had. I could keep trusting Him or die hurting and denying Him. I decided to keep trusting Him. I had already tried the alternative. Now, I wanted to finish the race.

*Being confident of this very thing, that He who has begun a good work in you will complete it until the day of Jesus Christ* (Philippians 1:6).

I accepted the path that had begun seven hours after death came to my home for my child. She was with the Lord; and even now, my life was being made new and different.

When I was sitting on the couch in the room holding Madison, I thought about everything. I remember sitting there and recalling a moment I had in the shower. I was meditating on Romans 8:28–39. Going over the Scripture, confirming God's love for me. Telling myself, *if God be for me, who can be against me?*

He gave His only Son so that I could be free and have what God wants for me. He gave His Son for me. That's love. He loves me and will answer all of my prayers. I just played the Scripture over and over in my mind—He gave His Son for me. He did that for me. I could not imagine doing that, but for me, God did it.

I began to consider just how deep that sacrifice was. I thought of the pain in God the Father's heart and the strength of determination for Jesus to take that mantle upon Himself.

I thought how selfless it was to give up so much for others. Others that fail to even live up to their potential. Others that fail to humble themselves and allow His glory to rise in them and conquer the very thing that wants to destroy us. I then heard:

*"You will know the pain of that sacrifice."*

It felt as if someone suddenly smacked me in my face. I shook myself to shake off the sting. I instantly rebuked the voice and told myself it was the enemy trying to create doubt.

I shouted: "The devil is a liar, and let every Word of God be true!"

Now, sitting in this room holding the body that once belonged to my beloved child, I thought, *maybe it was God. Maybe He'd been telling me this all the time. Maybe it was for a higher purpose. Maybe this sacrifice is not just about me, but others, too.*

But I did not love others the way God did. I did not care at that moment about anybody else. I knew only this: my baby was gone. And whether God or the devil said it, I was hurting, and I desperately needed things to make sense.

## Chapter Eight

*Arise, Shine ...*

*But the salvation of the righteous is from the Lord; He is their strength in the time of trouble. And the Lord shall help them and deliver them; He shall deliver them from the wicked, and save them, because they trust in Him. (Psalm 37:39–40)*

IT WOULD HAVE BEEN SO easy to walk away from God at that moment. I thought, *in spite of everything I thought and did, I still lost my baby.* It felt like I had no hope, and I questioned everything. *In spite of everything I believed, I was still in despair. God on my side did not seem to make a difference.* Those thoughts swirled around in my head constantly. I could have believed my feelings and decided that God doesn't answer prayers. I could have believed that no matter what we pray for or desire, it may never be because somewhere life is already written and the odds are stacked against us. That this "God thing" was a waste of time. The inevitable was the inevitable.

The trouble with taking that road was that I already knew God and knew that that mind-set was a lie. It was a hope of the enemy, for me to blame God for the bad and believe the enemy has all the power. But God already spoke to me. He was and had been with me all the time, and I knew it. The loss I faced did not change what I knew. He told me and showed me in dreams and visions that this was a faith fight. I had given my life to God. I had shut the door on fear, strife, and condemnation and the enemy was determined to test me in my truth, hoping I would fall and not get up.

*Deny* His existence or presence in my life? *No.* Not only had God been with me through this trial; but all the years *before* I got it, He constantly revealed His presence in my life, putting His fingerprint on my life. Even when I was a young child, God had demonstrated His power in my life. He knew this was going to happen, and that is why He kept showing Himself to me, so that I would not give up when the enemy showed up in my life in the worst way.

When I began writing this, I thought about the predestination of God (Jeremiah 1:4–10). He established me in relationship with Him before I was born. As my Creator, He knew me so well, my mistakes and achievements, my weaknesses and strengths. He breathed the breath of life into me, knowing frailties, likes, and dislikes. He knew how to orchestrate my life and knew what my response would be to the symphony He had written to be played out in my life.

We often justify our denial of the existence of God or our rebellion to His ways based on what we perceive to be His inactivity in our lives or refusal to grant us our way. This mind-set only proves that we understand neither God nor His Word. We usually have been, for the most part, operating in third-party hearsay and heresy, which is experiential, not factual.

We have not known the Word of God, and we have not had the mind of God, because many of us have never given our full attention to the Word of God—to read it, study it, meditate on it—so that it could be revealed to us. We have taken parts of His Word and applied them to our lives to satisfy our need to justify our own plans, but we have not taken the whole Word and applied our lives to it for its transforming effects. We have yet to seek the kingdom of God first or even know what that really means.

When things don't work out our way, we begin to doubt God and believe that this God thing—this faith thing—is not trustworthy or is just too complicated. So ... we hold on to what we know—fear, doubt, confusion, and the visible— what we see. We decide people are more dependable and, if they fail, it is understandable; they are not supposed to be perfect the way a never-failing God should be. We just can't accept disappointment from God—disappointment being that God failed to meet our expectations.

But God doesn't fail. So what makes us believe that God has failed us? I realize that we often feel this way because we see with human eyes, which cannot see what God sees. Because we have emotions—blinding feelings that block out communication from and communion with God, Who knows all and desires only the very best for us. It appears as failure because we make it about us, what we think, what we want, what we need for us, us, us. And God is not our servant. We belong to Him, we belong to each other.

God told me that I must first read the Word for myself. Pray for wisdom and understanding before, during, and after I read, which allows the Holy Spirit to give me understanding and the ability—the power—to move in the wisdom being revealed to me through God's Word. His Word transforms and strengthens faith. With faith strengthened I could begin to really see the face of God—the face I could trust—and would receive the coveted relationship I desired. Once in relationship with Him, I would understand Him and then myself. From this awakening, the truth of all things would be revealed. I would see that not only is God not a lie, but I would see the truth of myself also.

As life goes on, the foundation of my faith would be fortified as what I read became my reality, watching God do what He has said in His Word, working in my situation and through my issues to aid me. Through all things I would be strengthened to hold on until the final act of whatever the current drama was in my life. in obeying the Lord, I would take the power away from the situations in my life and acknowledge the power of God in my life and His willingness and ability to act in His power on my behalf.

I want to emphasize reading God's Word for yourself. Yes, God gives us pastors, prophets, and teachers to interpret and bring light to the Word for us. But like the Bereans (Acts 17:10–12), we must search the Scriptures for ourselves to know whether what we are being told is so. The Scriptures can be distorted, and personal agendas can be advanced through false teachers and ignorant, well-meaning people.

Having established regular reading and study of the Word and applying it to our daily living, what we then hear from others will either ring true in our spirit (1 John 4:1) or we will have a "dis-ease" in our spirit. We must ask God to grant us a discerning spirit (1 Corinthians 12:10), so that we may operate in the truth of God and know His voice, even when it is through a third party. And so, we read God's Word for truth and to discipline our own spirit for the service for which we were created.

I stated before that God had set me apart years before this occurred. I did not know it then, but God wanted me to know that not only did He exist, but that He was also as powerful and amazing as His Word states. I believe God revealed Himself in my life early so that I could never really walk away from Him. No matter how ugly things appeared to be, I could not deny Him. He knew me, and that is why

He made Himself so real to me. He knew that I would come up with these preconceived ideas as a child and build on them as I got older. He knew this loss was going to happen to me and that is why He established a presence in my life consistently in different ways. So no matter what, I could not deny Him.

As a child at around eleven years old, I received the Holy Ghost. I was not trying. The elders of the church would make us tarry for the Holy Ghost. It was never a desire on my part. I just went through the motions because it was expected. I was actually scared to receive the Holy Ghost. I was apprehensive of all things spiritual. It was too much like the boogeyman, haunting ghosts, and all the other unknowns we fear.

Whenever there was a tarrying service, I always focused on the terrifying screams and breath blowing in my face. Folks were spitting all over the place, and it was greatly disturbing to me. Instead of praying for the Holy Ghost, I was praying spit would not go in my mouth. I was not looking to get anything out of all this tarrying; I was too busy hoping they would hurry up and get this over with so I could go home. I would think to myself, *I am tired, and these hypocrites are getting on my nerves.*

In spite of my lack of concentration and my focus on running my mouth in church (hey! I was only eleven), God still managed to do His job, and I received the baptism of the Holy Spirit. *You did not choose me, I chose you"* (John 15:16).

I had already said the words and gone through the motions, and one Sunday I was sitting in the church pew yakking with a friend and half listening to the sermon, but engulfed in the music and emotion of the service, clapping my hands—when *bam!* I was dancing and screaming. Heaven knows I tried to fight it, but the sense of the whole thing was not only powerful, but amazing. I became conscious of what was happening, and it was mind-blowing. To feel as if you've lost yourself and have no control over your own body was definitely different for me and very intimidating in and of itself. But, at the same time, remaining conscious of this world and everything around you while being overtaken by the presence of the Spirit of God was miraculous!

I've never done drugs, but I promise you that there is no greater high than that overwhelming presence of the Holy Spirit. I've overdone the alcohol a time or two, and I can assure you that an alcohol buzz is nothing compared to what happened with the Holy Ghost. It is indescribable ... the pinnacle of the culmination of ecstasy. The Spirit of God had gained total control of me. I did not know whether to be frightened or excited. I think I was both. Afterward, I still tingled all over and felt as if I were floating. It is the clearest and cleanest high anyone could ever experience. I wanted it to never end.

The thought that at that moment God had chosen me (predestination—Rom. 8:29) and that I would let it be so (foreknowledge —1 Peter 1:2) was a real revelation to me. It was also a fearful revelation because I wondered, *what now? What happens to me now? What is expected of me now? How will others view me now? Would my friends wonder about me? Would adults expect something great and perfect from someone so blessed as to have received this gift so young? What if I can't live up to their expectations? What if God will not allow me to live down to my friends' expectations? What does this mean?*

It was a lot for an eleven-year-old kid to take in. Over and over I would be touched by the Holy Spirit for a long period of time. After awhile, I stopped trying to anticipate or fight against it. I gave into those visitations because nobody was giving me grief about it and no one put more expectations on me the way I thought they would.

Well, guess what? That all changed when I went to a district revival where all the churches of our denomination in the city got together. I was a part of the youth choir. We were singing and, of course, the choir and music were hypnotic. The church started to rock, and the kids were all up clapping and rocking with the music, engulfed in the excitement.

A man from my church was shouting and running around the church. He was near my row, and it seemed as if I could sense the Holy Spirit all over him, telling him to stop. Sure enough, the man suddenly stopped at the end of my pew, and he pointed in my direction. The presence of God was in the air, and I knew the Holy Ghost was on the move. It was as if I could literally see the Holy Spirit surrounding him like a tornado; and in the wind of the tornado I could hear, *I am coming for you.*

I closed my eyes thinking, *if I don't look, it won't happen.* I rehearsed the thought of me being embarrassed in front of schoolmates who were sure to tell everybody at school what happened. I could hear the taunts of "sanctified holy roller."

I opened my eyes to see if the gentleman from my church was still there and almost like a magic act, it happened. The man raised his arm and faced my direction. His arm was shaking, along with his body, as if he were having a seizure. When he lifted his arm in my direction, it was like lightning went through the air, and I was hit. I could not stop it. I could not even slow it down. It was so intense. It was a lot more intense than I had ever experienced before. I was captivated, and I loved every second of it.

Every thought went out of my head, and I was overcome with the desire to please God with my praise. I began to thank Him and thank Jesus. I began to praise God with my whole self. I felt special and wonderful all over. It was a magnanimous portion. But as it began to subside, I remembered where I was and thought, *oh my goodness*. I knew there were at least twenty students from my school at the revival. I knew I would be the topic of lunchroom conversation the next day.

The "next day" was still far away, and it had already started. We hadn't even left the sanctuary when a boy from my school came up to me laughing and pointing. He teased me about being sanctified and filled with the Holy Ghost and some other stuff. Then the other kids hanging around us started laughing along with him.

"Who do you think you are?"

"What were you doin', girl, fakin'?"

"She was fakin', y'all. She was not for real."

I was the butt of the joke, and I did not know how to handle it. I could handle criticism and ridicule, but not when it came to God and my relationship with Him. I did not know how to defend what was beautiful to me, but was being used to make me feel like an idiot. To believe in the invisible God and be one of those that dare to feel the intangible was and still is deemed foolishness, even by many believers. How do you defend yourself without looking like one of those crazy Jesus people? I did not have an answer, not even after such a wonderful encounter with God. I was crushed and confused.

I wanted to be accepted by the kids at school. School was tough enough for a nice-looking virgin with strict parents, who was not allowed to do what the other kids did, go where other kids went, or hang out where other kids hung out. I was not like them, and my parents weren't like theirs. Many of the parents that went to our churches still allowed their children to do whatever and go wherever. This experience should have been a good thing for me, and later on, I would embrace it as such, but at the time it made me an outcast.

I would once again be branded as "that girl."

"That girl's cute, but she will not give any play," said the boys.

"She dresses nice, but she's always in skirts, dresses, and pumps … Little Miss Uppity," said the girls.

I was that girl, who could not receive calls or company if her parents weren't home. That girl, who thinks she is cute and thinks she is smart and thinks this or that.

Every time I tried to *not* be that girl, I got caught in some mess with the kids I was trying to get in with. I got in trouble, while the troublemakers got away scot-free. I shouldn't have cared what the other kids thought, but I was after all a kid myself, so I thought and acted like a kid.

I guess I am being hard on myself thinking that at eleven years old, I should have been satisfied with the fact that I was deemed acceptable to God despite imperfections and lack of knowledge. Thinking I should have been able to rest in the appreciation that my persecution compared to Christ's persecution was miniscule and, therefore, I should've let it go. But I was a kid, and that did not compute. So, I forgive myself. After all, God knew what He was doing. It was all part of the orchestration of my life's symphony.

The teasing and taunting were wounds that hurt. Those I held to be my equals were shaming me for their own enjoyment and because of their own ignorance. Like any other child, I needed to know and to prove that I was okay. Kids often compare themselves with others to achieve some comfort within. To discover that we are different, not because of different hair or facial features, but because we are marked by God and set apart, doesn't make life any easier in a child's mind. For those children like me, surrounded by tainted superficial religious believers that can make an adult's walk difficult, their offspring make it hell. They feel justified in humiliating you and crushing your spirit because they themselves have yet to be taught or made to feel whole in their own household, where they profess to know and walk something they have yet to fully embrace or understand.

We can dye our hair and change our features, but we cannot change God or His plan. We are what He has said about us before time began (predestination), and He knows we will submit (foreknowledge)—eventually—and do what we were created to do. God demonstrated His power through His Holy Spirit, and I found this truth to be self-evident. It is His will and I can only submit myself to God's will or spend my life in rebellion.

What to do to arrest the mockery I endured at school? Well, in my ignorance, I tried to take control and halt the laughter by deflecting the matter. I became like Peter and denied the truth.

I yelled back at the church boy, "No, I am not, that man did something to me! It was him!"

After I said it, a crushing pain in my stomach penetrated through to my spine, and I felt even worse. I had just denied God and His blessing to be accepted by people I did not really know or like much. I denied my relationship with the Lord for knuckleheads who apparently did not care enough about me to think about how their belittling impacted me.

He and his buddies had felt it necessary to race across the sanctuary in an effort to knock me off an imaginary pedestal they'd created in their minds, and I fell for it. I understood how Peter must've felt. I had denied God; I had denied Christ. For what? For who?

I tried to come back from my comment and acknowledge God and His gift without looking too holy, but my tongue got tied and I did not know what to say, so I just walked away.

Instantly I began asking God to forgive me. I rationalized in my head what happened, while trying to convince myself that God understood. It did not help. I felt unbearably awful. What I did not know then, was that God uses the plot of the enemy and even our failures in His ultimate plan to project us toward our destiny.

After Peter's denial of the Lord Jesus and after the crucifixion, Jesus returned and visited His disciples. Jesus met with Peter and other disciples at the Sea of Tiberias, where Peter and the others were fishing. They had gone back to their former careers as fishermen.

> *… They went out and immediately got into the boat, and that night they caught nothing. But when the morning had now come, Jesus stood on the shore; yet the disciples did not know that it was Jesus. Then Jesus said to them, "Children, have you any food?" They answered Him, "No." And He said to them, "Cast the net on the right side of the boat, and you will find some." So they cast, and now they were not able to draw it in because of the multitude of fish. Therefore that disciple whom Jesus loved said to Peter, "It is the Lord!" Now when Simon Peter heard that it was the Lord, he put on his outer garment (for he had removed it), and plunged into the sea. But the other disciples came in the little boat (for they were not far from land, but about two hundred cubits), dragging the net with fish. Then, as soon as they had come to land, they saw a fire of coals there, and fish laid on it, and bread. Jesus said to them, "Bring some of the fish which you have just caught"* (John 21:3).

Since Jesus' betrayal and death, the guilt of Peter's denial had left Peter empty and ashamed. When Peter made the statement that he was going fishing, the translation was that he was going *back* to his former career in the fishing industry. He went back to his old ways, to what came naturally, and turned away from his purpose because of hurt, shame, loss, and disappointment in the situation and in himself.

Yes, he had seen the post-resurrection Jesus. But Peter's guilt and shame did not allow him to get the message from Jesus in John 20:21–23 when the Spirit of God was breathed onto the disciples and Jesus gave authority to forgive.

I realize that shame and unforgiveness in our lives stick with us. If we do not have a come to Jesus moment and forgive others and ourselves, we will perpetuate our unforgivenss and move back into a place from which we have been delivered. Persecution, the feeling of failure, hurt and loss can tempt us to backslide into our wrong, but familiar comfort zones.

Jesus engaged Peter in a series of three questions, which did three things: 1) caused Peter to consciously and verbally acknowledge where he was with Jesus; 2) caused Peter to know that, regardless of how Peter perceived himself, he had a purpose, a responsibility for others, and would be held accountable; and 3) caused Peter to know that in time, his relationship with Jesus would transform to become what it should be, and that the past mistakes, fear, and confusion did not negate that relationship or Peter's purpose.

I had to realize like Peter, that before I lost my child, I was on a road of strength, power, forgiveness and truth. I was in a relationship with God that was freeing and full of love and hope. God chose me for such a time as this and nothing changed God's mind or plan about me or my destiny. My situation and outside influences did not change the God Who had not and does not change His mind. When He chose me, He already knew my capabilities and my shortcomings.

God's love is constant—it cannot change—just as the love of our parents doesn't change, no matter how off-track we become. They become upset with us because they know we can do better—they know our potential—so out of love, they stay on us to live up to our potential and surpass it to fulfill a greater destiny. I was and am greater than I thought, and others saw that more clearly than I.

Peter saw for himself that despite his shortcomings, the love of the Lord was still intact and had not been shattered or destroyed by Peter's denial of Jesus nor Peter's denial of his destiny by going back to fishing. This was a lesson at age eleven that would come back to my remembrance at age thirty.

*When they had finished eating, Jesus said to Simon Peter, "Simon son of John, do you truly love me more than these?" "Yes, Lord," he said, "you know that I love you." Jesus said, "Feed my lambs." Again Jesus said, "Simon son of John, do you truly love me?" He answered, "Yes, Lord, you know that I love you." Jesus said, "Take care of my sheep." The third time he said to him, "Simon son of John, do you love me?" Peter was hurt because Jesus asked him the third time, "Do you love me?" He said, "Lord, you know all things; you know that I love you." Jesus said, "Feed my sheep"* (John 21:15-17).

Was Peter frustrated because Jesus had asked three times, "Do you love me?" In the original Greek, Jesus' first two questions used the Greek *agape*—"do you love me unconditionally to the ultimate?" Peter's response was, "I *phileo* you"—I love you like a friend"—"You my boy."

The third time, Jesus drops it to Peter's level. "Do you *phile* Me?"—"do you love me as a friend?" Peter is distressed for two reasons: 1) Jesus has made it clear now that He is willing to be loved by Peter at whatever level he chooses to love Him; 2) whatever level Peter's love is on, Peter still has a purpose, a responsibility, and will be held accountable for fulfilling that purpose and carrying out that responsibility.

I knew that God loved me and was willing to meet me where I was and walk me to the place I needed to be. He did it for me as a child and I knew He would do it for me in my pain of loss. In my confusion and disappointment, He would do it for me.

God did just that. He walked me out of despair once again. He met me at my river of tears and the loss. The place I seemed to go back to when things did not make sense. Like Peter, for a moment, I could not say I loved the Lord, not the way He desired, not the way I desired. I was perplexed, in pain, lost in anguish and could not say, "I love you," with all of my heart. I had been in this position a few times, but thank God, He and I both decided that this would be the last time I would ever be at this river, it was time for me to stick to the road He had carved for me. I was to leave this place forever and not to come back.

Jesus then gives Peter a Word of prophecy:

*I tell you the truth, when you were younger you dressed yourself and went where you wanted; but when you are old you will stretch out your hands, and someone else will dress you and lead you where you do not want to go." Jesus said this to indicate the kind of death by which Peter would glorify God. Then he said to him, "Follow me!"* (John 21:18)

Jesus indicated that eventually Peter would come to a place where he would love Jesus more than anything—even to the point of death. And Peter did. At approximately the age of eighty-four, Peter was crucified in Rome. His love for Christ was such that he requested to be crucified upside down because he did not feel worthy to be crucified in the same way his Savior had been crucified. I would eventually experience this turn around myself. Honesty, there were moments during my dejection it did not seem possible, but now I know better.

The Lord was saying to Peter, to me (to all of us), that I needed to do what I had been called to do. Shortcomings, failure, and guilt can stop us from progressing to our destiny if we do not deal with them through confession, repentance, and allowing the forgiveness and restoration of God to take place in our lives. I had to learn from my mistakes. I may have messed up in many different ways, but I still had purpose. I must allow God to do what He needs to do inside and through me, and move forward. My hurt and misunderstanding at the moment did not stop my journey; it was not a way out of what I had been called to do or be in this life. It was only a part of my completion.

*Peter turned and saw that the disciple whom Jesus loved was following them. (This was the one who had leaned back against Jesus at the supper and had said, "Lord, who is going to betray you?") When Peter saw him, he asked, "Lord, what about him?"* (John 21:20).

My concern is not to worry about others and the conversation *they* have had with God. I am only concerned with God's expectations of me, and how God will work in me to fulfill His plan.

I had to realize that God had not failed. Peter thought he failed, he had believed in Christ only for Christ to die as a common criminal. I know he asked just like I asked, How could he die, how is that bringing victory and restoration? I wondered how Madison's death would do the same.

His disappointment in God and himself took him to a place of familiarity. A place of disillusion, a place of uncertainty. But in that place Jesus showed up and showed Peter love when he could not love Jesus back. He gave Peter forgiveness and the promise of restoration and completion in his spirit and understanding.

God took me back over my life many times to show me that he had never left me, He showed me that I was His beloved and even when I left Him he waited for me to come back. He loved me and I was forgiven by the blood of Jesus (1 John 1:6–10) for everything—both real and imagined. He let me know that everything happens for a reason and no matter what the reason I was presently on track. It was my time -So, arise! Shine!

## Chapter Nine

# *Your Light Has Come!*

*I waited patiently for the Lord; and He inclined to me, and heard my cry. He also brought me up out of a horrible pit, out of the miry clay, and set my feet upon a rock, and established my steps, He has put a new song in my mouth—Praise to our God; Many will see it and fear, and will trust in the Lord. (Psalm 40:1–3)*

AFTER THE LOSS OF MY daughter, I thought about my life and why God had imprinted Himself so early on my life. I wondered why He made Himself so real, why He seemed so near and why did He later allow me to feel so abandoned after I dared enter into relationship with Him?

I cried out to Him repeatedly for clarity. Not because He had not already spoken to me, but for those times when I did not feel whole. Understanding did not always fill the emptiness, and I thought that the understanding should do just that. Other times I needed God to reiterate what He'd already said in order to soothe my soul and neutralize my carnal self so that I would know I was not operating in my own imagination. I needed Him to bolster and strengthen my faith to hold out for completion of this journey in anticipation of restoration.

Thoughts plagued me: *If this was not punishment, what kind of growth process was this? Why kill a child for the sins of the parent? If You are the God of love, why do I feel so unloved*

111

*and judged? If I have humbled myself before You and closed the door on fear, condemnation, strife, and so forth, why did this still happen? If You told me it would be all right and that You answer prayer, why did You not heal her? Why was my will for her not part of Your will? Is it not Your will to choose life? If this was to bring victory and you glory, Lord, how was that achieved? She's gone.*

Going through this over and over again, I finally concluded that having His promise, being in His presence, and being filled with His love doesn't stop hurt—it keeps us from dying spiritually and physically and mentally from the hurt. It doesn't stop the loss, it helps us through it. We will suffer in this life. Everyone will die—we can't stop that train from coming. But we *can* choose how we handle the ride, and we can choose the train stop.

*These things happened … as examples and were written down as warnings for us, on whom the fulfillment of the ages has come. So, if you think you are standing firm, be careful that you don't fall! No temptation has seized you except what is common to man. And God is faithful; he will not let you be tempted beyond what you can bear. But when you are tempted, he will also provide a way out so that you can stand up under it* (1 Cor. 10:11–13).

I recall the story of Adam and Eve's sons, Cain and Abel. When Adam and Eve were cast out of the Garden of Eden, God told the serpent that the seed of Eve would bruise his head, professing that out of Eve would come the one to defeat the same serpent that had tricked her into eating of the tree, thus sinning. She had promise that through her, things would be made right. She had the power of restoration and healing in her seed. After the loss and problems with the babies before Madison, I felt Madison was my promise—the completion and blessing after all the pain.

When Eve had Cain and Abel I am sure she believed that Cain and Abel were her blessings. However, instead of things getting better, Cain killed Abel. She had lost not only one son, but both sons. Cain had to be sent away marked as a murderer, and her other son was dead. I can imagine how Eve must have felt, when she was holding a promise of restoration and redemption in her spirit, only to discover that her son's blood cried out from the earth—and the culprit was her other son. This was not a promise come true, this was a nightmare where she had seemingly lost everything, including her promise, her hope.

I understood perfectly how she must have felt. Madison was my miracle, how could this end like this? How could this be? Where was the fulfillment of the promise? Why was I holding a body and not my baby? How was this all right? How was God in this?

I can imagine Eve asking if her past failure caused her current situation— asking, "Am I still being punished? I thought that was done and over. Has my sin continued to birth hell in my life? Where is the promise, where is the redemption?" I asked the same questions.

Sometimes life hits us so hard, we can often feel defeated.

*We are hard-pressed on every side, yet not crushed; we are perplexed, but not in despair; persecuted, but not forsaken; struck down, but not destroyed* (2 Corinthians 4:8–9).

In each of our lives we will have such a moment. There will be at least one time where something so crushing happens to us that we wonder if everything we believe, everything we were ever taught, was a lie. At least once in our lives, we will question our own faith in our own belief system and feel as if we are going crazy. As if we are losing our minds.

Nothing will make sense, and God along with everyone else will seem so far away. We will feel so disconnected from truth that everything in us screams out in despair because we feel so alone, so perplexed. It is a fresh pain and no one else we know will have felt our pain, will know our confusion, or will truly be able to understand or give us any real guidance or comfort. What is worse is that the same One we question will be the only one we will have—God. This was my dilemma. This is where I was. I walked in Eve's pain and confusion. I felt her emptiness.

I was faced with a defining moment that felt more like a disaster moment. It was a mess so big I did not know where to start to clean it up. I had no clue as to how to make things right, because I was in a truly unimaginable place, a place I never envisioned. It was a time when my situation did not match the promise or prophecy I trusted.

I thought, *if this is how it was going to be, if this is all it was ever going to amount to, then God lied. But how can He lie?* God is not a man, that He should lie or change His mind. So am I crazy? Did I not get it right? Who is talking to me? Who is with me? Am I making my own dreams, visions, promises? What am I looking at, and why does it seem so real? *Am I crazy?*

No one told me that life was going to be easy. They sure did not tell me that life could hurt so bad that it would contradict my being. What was I to do? What were my options when all I wanted to do was give up because tomorrow seemed too hard to face? What could I do when my life was such a contradiction I did not know if I was coming or going? What was I to do when I just wanted to give up trying to do either? I felt like I may have been crazy but my crazy world was more real than everything else? What am I to do when what I know makes more sense than what I see? When my situation, my circumstance doesn't jibe with what I know? Maybe my world is crazy? I thought, maybe it is something with me?

*I consider that our present sufferings are not worth comparing with the glory that will be revealed in us* (Romans 8:18).

I had to believe more was coming. I could not quit.

Jeremiah wanted to quit when the pressure was on. He was led by God, but persecution was on every hand. His walk and trust in the Word God had spoken to him appeared to bring more hell than peace. But since the Word was already written on his heart, he did not faint. Jeremiah faced challenging times which would have taken a lesser man out. Murder attempts, jail time…despair as he prayed for his people. But God brought him through and proved His Word in Jeremiah.

It is almost impossible to turn away from God's truth. Sure, we look crazy for the moment, but there is something about the Word of God that we cannot walk away from once we have drank from its rivers. Where would we turn to? What would we believe in? Where else can we go?

*O Lord, You induced me, and I was persuaded; You are stronger than I, and have prevailed. I am in derision daily; everyone mocks me. For when I spoke, I cried out; I shouted, "Violence and plunder!" Because the word of the Lord was made to me a reproach and a derision daily. Then I said, "I will not make mention of Him, nor speak anymore in His name." But His word was in my heart like a burning fire shut up in my bones; I was weary of holding it back, and I could not* (Jeremiah 20:7–9).

I held on to what God had shown and told me. I held out for fulfillment of the promises. There was something not complete about my situation. There had to be more to this. Where was my redemption, my restoration, my resurrection?

During this time of my life, I often dreamed that I was in the military. Always in uniform, in or near a field of battle or walking around the campsite. Sometimes I sat in the bleachers waiting for instructions with the other soldiers.

The day before Madison passed I had a dream that I was called out of those bleachers. I had Madison with me. We crossed over some water to what seemed like another military or refugee camp. Soldiers everywhere.

The place appeared to be secluded. I kept wondering where I was and if I was still a soldier. Why was I here? And if I was a soldier, why was my child with me walking around? I walked into a tent, and it was more like a room or bay area. There was a woman standing at the door when I walked in. With her hands folded, she stated, "We have been waiting on you."

As far as the eye could see from end to end, side to side, were baby beds. The inside of the tent was all white; it did not look like a military tent inside as it did outside. There were a few babies in beds, but most were empty. They all had names and gifts in the beds. The stitch from my surgery from earlier in the week from a second ectopic pregnancy I had during Madison's illness was hurting from carrying Madison, so I laid her in one of the beds.

She just looked around and did not say anything. The lady at the entrance who had said she had been waiting on us came over to show me Madison's bed. She was dressed in all white, sort of like the old Catholic nurses' uniforms—white long dress, white hat. She had something around her neck that made me think of a cross, but I am not sure what it was. She walked with folded hands before me down a long aisle to Madison's bed.

As I walked down the aisle, I noticed all the beds had names, dates, and numbers on the beds and on the clothing in the beds. The clothing also had foreign symbols on it. I did not understand the imprint on the clothes at all. I got to Madison's bed, and my belly was in pain; so I laid her down and leaned into the bed with her. I went through all the gifts in her bed. All the clothing were red and dark blue. I started looking around for clues of what this meant. I was waiting for someone to come and say something to me. *Was I to leave her here?* I wondered. *Is this it, is she not coming back, or is this the place of her healing?* I began to analyze everything, looking for a sign to tell me something.

The colors—I thought red for the blood, maybe the cleansing and healing. He will let her stay. He has to. I thought, purple and blue usually mean ultimate reward, which would make me wonder that he was saying she is passing, but I have never heard of red and blue being ultimate reward, passing. Then I noticed there was a number 3 on all of her stuff, and that made me wonder. I could not make out the symbols, but her name was on everything.

Then I noticed her date was blank. I thought, *Thank you, God, she is not staying here. She is staying with me.* I looked at Madison in my own glee, and she looked at me like *poor mom, you don't get it.* And I did not get it, because I did not want to get it. Suddenly sadness came over me, and tears began to roll down my face. I wanted to ask questions, but I feared the answers. The weight of the sadness was too real, too heavy already. I wanted to hold out faith for what I wanted; I did not want anyone to say anything contrary, so I tried to make myself believe what I wanted in hopes it would make it so. I continued to talk to her and went through her things while the tears rolled. Madison just looked at me. I later realized that the date was blank for my sake, but the date was well-established. The next day, Madison was gone.

Thinking on the dream I would tell myself, *God will take care of her. He showed me that she would be taken into the care of those taking care of all of his children in the Army of the Lord.* Not long after that, I was lying in bed thinking and crying as usual, and I heard Madison call to me from the hallway. I thought I had lost my mind. I froze in mid leap, thinking *is this a dream? I don't remember going to sleep. Did I just lose my mind?* I then hoped that I *had* lost my mind because I could live with hearing her voice, even if everybody thought I was crazy.

I heard her voice a second time, making her usual noises to let me know she was present. I opened the door to my bedroom and responded, "Madison? Is that you?"

A third time I heard her voice, "Mommy, Mommy! Can you hear me?"

I just began to cry because I could hear her, but I could not find her. I jumped up, and I ran down the hall from room to room, calling "Madison, Madison, where are you, baby? I can't find you. I hear you, but I can't find you!"

As I went past the kitchen and family room, the sunlight was so bright it fairly danced around the walls.

I heard her voice again. "Um, um, Mommy, they said I can't come there."

"I just want to see you," I pleaded.

I heard her voice say again, "They said I can't come. Um, I wanted to know if I, um, can come visit you sometimes."

I thought to myself, *no one is going to believe this. I can never tell anyone.* Everyone was waiting for me to crack, and now I had—but if this was what it was like to lose your mind, I could see why people do. At the time, it was the best medicine.

I answered, "Madison, come see me anytime, baby, I miss you so much. I love you so much. Please come see me anytime."

She kept talking and said, "okay, maybe like holidays or some days." I was so emotional with wanting to touch her so badly and she sounded so sweet and healthy.

For three days after this, I did not have any dreams of Madison, and it hurt. I missed her dearly, and the dreams I often had of her were helping me. Then I dreamed of two angels. They came and told me that Madison was all right. They took me to see her and let me hold her and play with her. While I was there, they told me secret things about my future and comforted me about my life, my path. I can't remember many specifics, I only remember the feeling I had and my responses, because I could not believe they were talking about me. I just kept saying, "Really, me, for me?" I do remember a child that was in my future that looked so much like Madison, just fatter. Madison was healthy and beautiful, like her old self—happy.

The place where the angels took me was a joyous place. The angels were fun and compassionate, and their presence filled me with joy, peace, and comfort. It was such a happy place. I did not want to leave. I was content and comforted not only being in that place, but seeing Madison and knowing she was healed and perfect. She was happy on the other side, she was loved, and she still knew and loved me. I would always be her mother. That's what I wanted, to always be her mother. To always love her, and she always to love me. I did not want death to take that, even if it took her body. I needed that. God blessed me with that.

I knew in my heart that my daughter was well taken care of in heaven with the Lord. In the dream I'd had, the nurses, the angels were taking care of everyone. There had been so much love and care in the tent and in the place I was able to visit Madison. I was at peace that she was all right. God blessed her, and she was enjoying her reward.

I tell you this, because I want you to know that God knows all things. He was prepared to receive her on the other side, and God was prepared to restore what I had lost. That room in my dream was filled to receive many others, not just Madison, and the dates let me know that He already knew what was going to happen and has everything taken care of for whoever goes.

This message is not limited to just suffering the loss of a person. When we allow God to fill the emptiness created by any loss, He restores us of whatever it is. He completes us and fills the vacancy. He brings us to the place He has predestined, and if we allow God to do it, He makes good on His Word and His promises, and we will have joy again.

Not long after that I had dreams of two little girls. One with curly hair and the other one with straight hair, one was also a little thicker than the other, but both reminded me of Madison – one more than the other. They were always in the front yard – which, in a dream, usually means that which is in your future. One day the two little girls took me to an upper room in a house next to my home and in the room was a huge kitchen. There was a table in the middle of this kitchen and a child was sitting at the head of the table. The two little girls sat at the table and a lady was teaching all three of the children different things.

I asked what was going on and was told that the children were being prepared to be born. One of the little girls turned around and smiled at me. Then she pointed to the other child at the head of the table, who was much younger than the two girls and she stated that he was not ready to be born yet, he is still learning. I felt hope when I woke from that dream. Could this be restoration? Would they be born to me? Were the little girls I had dreams of not Madison, but children yet to come. Was God showing me a promise of restoration through another birthing all along? Either way, I felt hope.

God restored Eve, and she had Seth. From Seth was the lineage that brought forth Jesus, and her hope was restored. Her promises had life once again. The enemy may think he has us down at any time. But I have evidence that his head was bruised as promised, so don't let him think for one second that he has won anything with us either.

We serve a God Who restores and will give us another chance at happiness, peace, joy, love, success. He will give us another blessing. He will restore us in every area we have lost. Try Him and trust Him again, and you will be victorious despite what today looks like. The loss was not the end, it was another beginning.

## Chapter Ten

### *Completion*

*"So I will restore to you the years that the swarming locust has eaten, The crawling locust, The consuming locust, And the chewing locust, My great army which I sent among you. You shall eat in plenty and be satisfied, And praise the name of the LORD your God, Who has dealt wondrously with you; And My people shall never be put to shame" (Joel 2:25–26).*

IN MY JOURNEY I LEARNED that God truly is the alpha and omega. The beginning and the end. When He showed me things, when He spoke, when He revealed things to me He always acted in the spirit of Alpha and Omega. Everything He showed, all that He said and revealed was in reference to the beginning and the end. The end of something ushering in the beginning of something else. He speaks of fulfillment and completion, the end of a thing. He speaks on perfection and wholeness, restoration and resurrection, the beginning and creation of a new thing.

He only sees His creation and calls it by the name He has given it, not the name of its process of becoming or what it used to be. God calls us by what we shall be according to His predestination. When Gideon was scared and disappointed, God called him a mighty man of valor. When Job called himself dejected and felt cursed, God said he was an upright and blameless man, when Jeremiah called himself a child, God called him a prophet.

Everything we go through is part of the journey He has already established to bring us into being what He calls us. I had to make it through to the other side of what I faced to reach completion. I had to learn to answer to the name God called me before the foundations of the world - His beloved.

It is important to persevere through every situation because that is the only way completeness in our being is achieved. My loss became my vehicle that brought me into the secret place of the Lord, in turn, it ushered me into His promise, His power, completion, newness and abundant life.

Moses told Pharaoh that the Lord wanted His people freed to sacrifice and worship Him in the desert. That desert would become a pit stop between Egypt and Canaan (the Promised Land), where they would learn and practice worshipping God. It was also a place where God would purge all the negative influence of slavery out of His chosen people.

Wilderness doesn't seem like the perfect plan in my book, and I—like the Israelites—thought that either God had abandoned me or maybe I did not get something right in the first place. Wilderness is a place to be delivered from, not into.

But God's plan always has purpose - to make us whole and to heal hurts of the past so that we can fulfill our purpose without the presence of a permanent distraction and disruption. To teach His people to trust, obey, and worship Him whether in the wilderness or the Promised Land. It is God's will to prepare you for His goodness so that you do not forget Him when you get to the high place, the place of destiny.

Of course, the Israelites failed to allow that preparation, and an eleven-day "pit stop" turned into home for forty years. But even in the desert, they received promises of abundance and restoration, and the Lord sustained them the entire time. However, their inability to adhere to the Word of God, their constant complaining, discontent, lack of praise, lack of worship, and lack of gratitude kept them from coming into the fullness of God's goodness, blessing, and favor.

*Save when there shall be no poor among you; for the LORD shall greatly bless thee in the land which the LORD thy God giveth thee for an inheritance to possess it: Only if thou carefully hearken unto the voice of the LORD thy God, to observe to do all these commandments which I command thee this day. For the LORD thy God blesseth thee, as he promised thee: and thou shalt lend unto many nations, but thou shalt not borrow; and thou shalt reign over many nations, but they shall not reign over thee* (Deuteronomy 15:4–6).

Don't let yourself get stuck in offense, anger, strife, "woe is me," malice, or unforgiveness, causing you to miss getting to the other side. Don't miss the promise and inheritance that is yours. Don't be satisfied with sustainment in the wilderness when overflow of the Promised Land is yours.

We want to be complete and whole in order to receive the blessing. We want to eliminate the shackles of the past so that we are not prevented from fulfilling our destiny. My spirit was purged, being rid of fear, frustration, disappointment, distorted doctrine, wrong philosophy, spiritual discontentment and the like. God was preparing and completing me.

What became evident to me during this time was that it is important for us to experience life's roller coasters and conquer the drops as well as relish the highs. Because in the end, this journey is not all about us. The "woe is me" attitude is not the answer, the right response is "Oh, let me get this right because it is important for other people, my family, my friends, my world as well as for me. May I be a light of victory and hope. May I get us closer to the Promised Land and not contribute to the wilderness experience." We must strive to be whole so that God can bless us and make us a blessing.

God, in the form of Jesus the Christ, became a human being for our sakes, so that when we pray and take our confusion, pain, distress, and all other destructive forces to Him in prayer, we can pray confidently with the knowledge that God *knows* what we are going through because He Himself has been through what we go through.

*For we have not a high priest which cannot be touched with the feeling of our infirmities; but was in all points tempted like as we are, yet without sin* (Hebrews 4:15).

Jesus knew His plight. He was there when His story was written, and yet, when the force of the pain weighed down on His soul and His flesh, He asked God if it could be taken away.

*And going a little farther, He threw Himself upon the ground on His face and prayed saying, My Father, if it is possible, let this cup pass away from Me; nevertheless, not what I will [not what I desire], but as You will and desire* (Matthew 26:39).

Jesus persevered for us. He could have stop it, changed it, not followed through, but it was not about Him, it was about us. It was important for Him to complete His mission and endure what was necessary for others to be made whole. Through His completion we are made complete. We learn to operate in this same spirit of understanding and purpose.

*That they all may be one, as You, Father, are in Me, and I in You; that they also may be one in Us, that the world may believe that You sent Me. And the glory which You gave Me I have given them, that they may be one just as We are one: I in them, and You in Me; that they may be made perfect in one, and that the world may know that You have sent Me, and have loved them as You have loved Me* (John 17: 21-23).

We learn that the purpose is bigger than the situation. In the process of pain, there is purpose; there is power coming forth and power being destroyed and overcome. I am in a spiritual battle, on a faith journey. I am in this with all of humanity. We are one in the Father, one in Christ.

As members of the Kingdom of God, our pain will be used to heal and serve others. Instead of passing judgment when others are going through things, we share, help and empathize because we've been there and know the hurt and pain and are able to enter into their grief.

The finest flour is used in the Holy of Holies. You may be sifted over and over, but it leads to perfection and the refining process produces the best end result. The more refined you are, the more precious you are to the kingdom.

Like Christ or a pregnant woman, we look beyond the suffering for the joy to come (Hebrews 12:2). I am obligated to fulfill my purpose, knowing that God has the victory over my battles already.

*I have told you these things, so that in Me you may have [perfect] peace and confidence. In the world you have tribulation and trials and distress and frustration; but be of good cheer [take courage; be confident, certain, undaunted]! For I have overcome the world. [I have deprived it of power to harm you and have conquered it for you]* (John 16:33).

The enemy has a plan to try to stop the progress of truth. He wants to stop us from making it to our destination. God has set this thing up so that each of us has an assignment and must do our part in order to fulfill, not only our individual purpose, but together fulfill the purpose of the whole counsel of God for the kingdom of God. In doing so, you will be greatly rewarded; don't get stuck in the process or distracted by the pain. The fight is fixed. We have already be slated to win. The victory is already ours. We only have to show up and do what God says.

For a short time, I thought I had messed up and did not wait on God. Maybe I jumped the gun or did something out of sync. Prayed wrong, confessed wrong, got too bold, or maybe not bold enough. I thought that maybe my faith was faulty and my understanding was wrong because my daughter died, but that was not so. I was going back over my life to see what I did to offend God and warrant this letdown in my relationship with the Lord, but that was a spirit of confusion and a lie.

Jesus still had to go to the cross, John the Baptist was still beheaded, Stephen was stoned to death. Paul faced more drama continuously than almost any other apostle or disciple. Their faith in God cannot be disputed. Sometimes life just happens. In my situation, it was life happening because life happens in this sinful world. But God used this situation to grow me and get me to a more intimate place in Him. I was brought closer to Him. To a place where I know what I know and cannot be shaken.

I trusted Him despite what I had gone through. I needed to consciously accept His will, no matter what, in all things and be willing to operate in that will utilizing the faith God has already supplied. I needed to get to a place where I would actually allow God to be *everything* for me and all that His Word says He would be in my life, no matter what. I needed to accept that God was God, regardless of the situation and how I got there.

The dreams, the visions were encouragement, God touching me, leading me so I would not get weary or distracted. Showing me my end. He needed me to keep going in order to finish the race in expectation of His promise. I had to complete the race to be made whole. He already knew that I would be all right and I would then know after it was over, that He is and will always be with me.

In the book of my life written by God, God had more for me to learn and more for me to receive than I understood or knew, but to receive it and be prepared for it, I needed to get through this *first*. I had to be prepared to receive. I needed to know Him, walk through the fire with Him, get upset, get over it and realize who He is and who I am in Him. I needed to be solid in the truth, I needed to be in a relationship in which there was no doubt because I knew too much about Him and I knew just as much about myself.

In the face of all that happened, understanding came, even when it seemed as if I were too cloaked in grief to fully receive. With God, we must sometimes simply trust Him (based on His track record with us) before we know or fully understand. God was dispensing wisdom, knowledge, and understanding all along the way to help me, to focus me, to comfort me, to transform me.

God flooding me with dreams, revelations, and visitations even after Madison's passing. But with all I had learned I was still not able to decipher all the details of the "road map" for this journey—only the possible beginning, the end, and participants in the situation. I was not aware of every detail presented (Prov. 1:5–7). But the Holy Spirit reveals much and those revelations were sufficient to keep me.

I trust Him enough to do whatever He says and go wherever He says, even if I do not fully understand right now at this moment why. It is, after all, the predestined path He knows, not the one we created. With Him we will surely be protected and warned, prepared for and protected from any upcoming dangers. I learned that God can meet us where we are and lead us to the place we need to be, without us having the directions ourselves. We trust His Word and His way because we know the possibilities of our tomorrow from His Word; even if we do not know where we are currently, He knows and will come and get us.

*It was by faith that Abraham obeyed when God called him to leave home and go to another land that God would give him as his inheritance. He went without knowing where he was going. And even when he reached the land God promised him he lived there by faith—for he was like a foreigner, living in a tent* (Heb. 11:8–9).

God walked me through understanding on my way to the manifestation of His will in me. God is not going to tell us everything. That is what faith is for, why we need to trust Him. He will not always give us a play-by-play. He gives us His Word, a promise, and light along the way as He directs us to the place of completion. Yes, it is all about faith.

*The LORD had said to Abram, "Leave your country, your people and your father's household and go to the land I will show you. I will make you into a great nation and I will bless you; I will make your name great, and you will be a blessing. I will bless those who bless you, and whoever curses you I will curse; and all peoples on earth will be blessed through you"* (Genesis 12:1).

Did Abraham question God to see if God knew what He was doing? Abraham simply obeyed and went. God did not tell Abraham where the land would be, how it would look, who else would be there, if it had a home on it, how it would happen, or anything else. Abraham walked out of his comfort zone in faith, down an unknown path with a promise. Abraham came from Ur, a place where people worshipped gods of stone. However, he acted on the voice of the invisible God that directed him to move on. That is called *faith*.

God's directions may at times appear weird. But I keep walking in faith and confidence of His promise. My faith is being exercised into perfection daily—not so that God can see anything, but for *me*. *I* need to know where my faith is and what kind of faith I possess. No need to think I have faith for a yacht, when I can't believe for a floating duck for my tub. Know where you are so that you know where you need to focus and perfect within yourself to manifest the fullness of God's purpose in your life.

Like Abraham, we will be called on at times to let go of all we know—tradition, ideologies, home, disappointment, doubt, fear, hurt, anger, pain, mediocrity, and imbalance— to go where the Lord leads and enter into the place for which God has given us an anointing.

## Chapter Eleven

### Job

*I tell you the truth, you will weep and mourn while the world rejoices. You will grieve, but your grief will turn to joy. A woman giving birth to a child has pain because her time has come; but when her baby is born she forgets the anguish because of her joy that a child is born into the world. So with you: Now is your time of grief, but I will see you again and you will rejoice, and no one will take away your joy (John 16:20–22).*

IN MY JOURNALING I WROTE a lot about Job, comparing our situations. I saw how God deals in seasons, and when our time—our season—has come, it may be ushered in through pain. When Jesus tells of His upcoming predestined victory over death, He uses the story about a woman giving birth. He speaks of when the woman's time of delivery has come she is in great pain, but the joy that comes after the birth overshadows the pain of the birthing process.

God wants us to know that what we deliver will give way to joy and reward greater than the pain we suffered. The suffering we endured will be forgotten for the joy of what has been brought forth. The stretch marks left by carrying the promise for a time and then bringing the life of God into our situation are well worth everything. We will say, "It was good for me. Look now at what great thing perseverance has brought forth."

Don't get me wrong, the pain of losing Madison was unspeakable and sometimes the thought of days past will cut through me all over again. Those days are not forgotten in the sense that they never come to mind. But restoration is taking place, the pain is dissipating, and the scars are healing. Because God is Who He is, the restoration of my joy was inevitable. Though the pain is still evident from time to time, more and more I am left less with tears and more with peace when I look upon the sweet memories of her existence.

Again, we are not released from life and what happens, including sorrow.

*Many are the afflictions of the righteous, but God will deliver us from them all* (Psalm 34:19).

But what we believe becomes what we experience. I choose to believe His Word, His promise of my restoration. *Let us not wallow in the emptiness … there is more for us on the other side of our trials, both here and now and in the spiritual realm. God has made promises for this life and the life after—eternal life.*

Job stated that even if God were slowly killing him, he would still serve Him. If anyone can attest to loss and hanging onto God's promise of restoration, it would be Job—and he was not under the New Covenant made perfect by Christ. How much more can we expect under the New Covenant?

Job lost all of his children, his business, and his influence. His wife could not stand for her husband to suffer so and desired for him to cut his losses, curse God, and die. All around Job was disillusion. On top of everything else, his health went south. All of this happened to a man that was pronounced righteous by God.

Job held on to faith in God even when he did not understand. If we come to God, believing that there is a God and that He rewards those who sincerely seek him (Heb. 11:6) He will show up. Our faith moves Him. The Lord is our help; let us not be afraid. God has always been with us, and though we walk through the valley of the shadow of death, we shall fear no evil for He is with us.

Often we feel like we are being slaughtered and losing the battle, but if we could just see behind the curtains, God is always in control. He was always in control of Job's situation, and He was always in control of my situation. God set the boundaries for the extent and intensity of Job's test. He also told the devil when to skedaddle, and the devil obeyed His command, because no matter what the enemy tries, God has the last say. God can override everything, but our giving up.

God is always in total control of our situation. Even when we are going through the unspeakable, know that He is there and will never leave us or forsake us. We are still here because whatever rose up against us was not allowed to kill us or destroy us. If the waters of the oceans go no further than where God has commanded and the devil responds in agreement to God's commands, then the turmoil in our life has a limit and will also obey the command of the Lord. All of our struggles "come to pass"—they do not stay and must conform to the will of God.

Whom God has blessed is blessed and whom God has cursed is cursed. We learn this through the story of Balaam and Balak. When God has blessed you the enemy cannot do anything to you. I am blessed and was and still am blessed because God said that I am. No matter what you are facing you are blessed because God said you are and your situation does not change what God has called you. No one can do anything to you, but the enemy can come in and try to cause you to destroy yourself in the midst of your situation through deception and playing on past weaknesses.

In Job 3:25, a long-standing fear of Job surfaces: the loss of the good life that came from God. He feared God, but Job did not know God. He served God and was grateful, but his fear of God's power and resulting loss of abundant life surpassed anything else. Job's relationship with God was based on works. He sacrificed to God not only for himself but his family also (Job 1:4-5) in the event they had sinned. So do many of us operate – in the fear only and not the love of the Lord. That is not relationship. Therefore, there is no perfect peace and no perfect love.

The enemy was hoping that Job's fear would play out in the reaction to his loss, that he would blame God, curse Him and die (spiritually). Job said a lot of things but the challenge was to get Job to curse God and that, Job did not do and so the enemy was unable to bring Job out of God's protection.

God used this situation to get what He wanted out of Job: a relationship based on the right thing – knowing God.

In my "Job time" I had to stay focused on what God said. I stayed focused on God. I chose to hear His voice over the voice of the enemy and looked past the picture the enemy had painted at that moment my baby left this earth. Just like Job, God led me through the wonder of Who He was – Creator, God, All Powerful, All Mighty, Counselor… He Who flung the stars into the universe and calls them by name…Who calls me Beloved.

I did what God said and said what God said and He did what He said He would do for me because that is how God is.

The enemy shows you the death of something hoping you will conform to what you see and death will become you, but you must choose life and faith and what was lost or stolen will be restored double back to you.

*I call heaven and earth as witnesses today against you, that I have set before you life and death, blessing and cursing; therefore choose life, that both you and your descendants may live; (Deuteronomy 30:19)*

To be cursed means that you have chosen to live without God, for God is love (1 John 4:7-8). You have chosen to live without the benefits of His love – favor, grace, blessing, mercy… you have chosen the empowerment to fail in life. To be blessed means that you have chosen to live in relationship with the Lord and all the rights, privileges and benefits thereof. You have chosen to walk with the authority given by God to succeed in life.

The Word of God mixed with faith and perseverance can overcome all things and bring life and the promised reward of blessing in all situations. Resurrection and restoration power. We have that power as a gift from God sealed by the death and resurrection of Christ Jesus Who redeemed us from the curse of the law (Galatians 3:13).

I chose life, the empowerment to win because I know I have been called to win in all things. Don't let the enemy name your situation for you and cause you to curse yourself. Call him a liar and instead say what God has said. Speak what God has told you to say, not what fear or frustration is selling.

Job stated "What I feared has come upon me; what I dreaded has happened to me" (Job 3:25). He was further confessing his fear. In this chapter Job recounts his turmoil and he cursed the day he was born. As Job received clarity from the Lord in the later chapters of Job, Job realized that he may not have cursed God, but he had yet to speak the word of the Lord over his life and situation. His focus had been on his misery, not on the Lord. When Job met God face to face in his situation he received revelation that fear and not faith were operating in his life and at that moment a change occurred. He then said to the Lord in chapter 40 teach me how to hold my mouth. This revelation could only be manifested through relationship and faith, not works.

Job moved from confusion and questioning God to asking God to show him how to speak. Job asked God to help him to shut his mouth and teach him how to walk in the Spirit and truth of God. Job realized there was more of God that he needed and wanted and changed his focus from his situation to God. He surrendered to the will of the Lord and said put your Word in my mouth.

We must understand that out of the mouth the heart speaks, so there was an actual revelation that Job needed a change of heart and wanted God to bring forth that transformation so that he would no longer walk in fear, but in relationship with the Lord. The enemy intended to exploit Job's weakness of relationship, but God used the attack of the enemy to draw Job nearer in covenant with Him. Relationship was the only thing that could bring forth even greater blessing and real peace in Job's seemingly perfect life. What the devil means for bad, God will always make for our good.

However, the comments of Job's friends made it look as if God had abandoned Job as a punishment. You would think from the condemnation of his so-called friends that Job had offended God and warranted severe punishment.

How often when we or others go through turmoil are words similar to those of Job's friends used to persecute the

Job

suffering? God himself states that Job was His servant, "the finest man in all the earth—a man of complete integrity. He fears God and will have nothing to do with evil."

In our human thinking of "cause and effect," we believe a person has to have done something to ignite God's anger and that suffering is always a result of God's anger for sin.

When we go through difficult situations, we not only go through them for ourselves, but for others. But we are set to triumph every time.

*Now thanks be to God who always leads us in triumph in Christ, and through us diffuses the fragrance of His knowledge in every place* (2 Corinthians 2:14).

God prepares us to serve others through our victory so that they too can be healed, and led out of darkness. Sometimes out of our hardships a trail is being blazed to lead others. In Job's case, he went through this because God knew that he would withstand the storm and bring glory to His name, setting a solid example for us thousands of years later.

I needed Job to strengthen my faith. Someone is going to need my story to carry them through. I need to encourage others to persevere because their story will heal someone else. It is never about us. We are not islands. All that we go through is part of a bigger picture. We impact the world in every decision we make. We sow seeds every second of the day. When we reap the benefits or consequences of those seeds, the world is impacted—and generations to come will be impacted as well. When we choose life, it spreads, if we choose death, it spreads as well. We are choosing not just for ourselves, but for others.

As Job was going through his trial, his friends agreed to go see him together and console him. That is great and is exactly what we should do for those going through trials.

For seven days they sat with him in silence, waiting for him to first respond. *Sometimes there is nothing that can be said.* His friends did not even recognize him and wept at the sight of him. After seven days Job spoke to them about what he was going through. He spoke through his emotions and pain.

Like all of us, wondering why so much had come against him, Job went through a plethora of emotional turmoil. *Why do right if we suffer the same fate as the wicked? Just kill me. I should have been stillborn or, better yet, not born at all.*

Like all of us, he wanted his friends to console him and reassure him that he was okay. Instead, they got all churchy on him and began to condemn him with the words and ways of God instead of staying on course to comfort their friend and encourage him.

I had to be careful about with whom I spoke while I was going through the ordeal with Madison. Out of the mouth pours life or death. I limited those I spoke with during this time. I did not want to hear pity, negativity, or assumptions from carnal minds or stories about someone else I did not know or care about at the moment. I was dealing with enough; I did not need anyone else's story or complication. I was dealing with my situation with the only one I needed, God and His Word.

If people came with conversations that attempted to pull me out of faith or strength or that were about what I did not want to hear, I could not stand it. People think they are doing you a favor by complaining or making statements lined with pity and sorrow, because they think that is what they would want if they were in your situation.

The best thing to say is nothing, like Job's friends started out, and wait to see what the person in the situation is saying. What is their tone? Allow their voice and feelings to be heard and let them lead you where they are - don't try to drag them where you think they should be. There are very few people who want pity or want people to act like they know what we are going through. Unless you have actually walked in the shoes of the very same situation, you do not know what we are going through and it feels as if it is being trivialized for the other person's comfort, not for the comfort of the one in the situation.

I loved having people call or visit if they were happy and uplifting, and spoke as if everything was fine and would be fine. They just wanted to see if they could do something to make life easier for me. They were not calling to dump a load on me. Just because I have a load doesn't mean I want to discuss my loads and yours as well. All the "oohs" and "ahhs" were horrible.

I understand exactly how Job felt. If you are going to make it worse or if you have come to cry with me, I don't want it. I can do bad all by myself. I need a break from the situation, not someone to come and bask in it so they can go away and tell everyone how great they were for me or to me, how they cried with me. Rebuke that!

Close family and a handful of friends were the limit. There were many that did not even know Madison had cancer until after she passed because I never told them. Protecting my faith, my heart, my hope, my mind, my word was more important to me. I knew I had to be focused to fight this faith fight. I needed the prayers and faith of those invested in my life to sustain me; I did not have time to console others about my situation.

Job's friends were exactly that burden. Instead of comforting him, they felt Job was arrogant to think he was special to God, and they brought condemnation on Job. There is nothing wrong in thinking highly of ourselves—we are blessed and highly favored of the Lord just don't think more highly of yourself than you ought to.

*For by the grace given me I say to every one of you: Do not think of yourself more highly than you ought, but rather think of yourself with sober judgment, in accordance with the measure of faith God has given you* (Romans 12:3).

I understand that Job felt special. I understood that when you know who you are and whose you are, you also know the inheritance and privileges that come with that and you are in expectation of that which you have been told is yours.

Like Job, we are special to God. We know the truth of His Word, and it lives in us. We hold on to the blessed reward and promises that come with being in relationship with God. We know what He has done for us, and we are grateful and feel blessed and highly favored. We should feel special enough for God to trust to show His glory through us. If you know who you are in God and you have the faith to back it up, be bold. Just make sure you don't get too far and fall into pride. Many times we don't even know we are arrogant. Thinking that we are above the law and "how dare this happen to me," can often come from a place of arrogance and pride, not confidence in a relationship with God.

There is a tendency to want God to follow the law of fairness, or whatever we consider justice. We lie to ourselves in our own self-importance, and out of our own imagination, we speak over the Word of God and begin to preach to God, "I am worthy and thus should have all things, when and where I desire, because I am that great." *Wrong!!!* Not only are we not that great, but there is a definite need for an attitude adjustment. We believe that God, if He is so good, will conform to the same law of fairness that we subscribe to, and in doing so, He will act accordingly. When He doesn't, we cry foul because according to our playbook, it is not fair and thus He is not God. That is arrogant because now we believe we are God and God is the servant that should abide by the principles we have established.

But God Himself is the standard of justice. He uses His power according to His own moral perfection. Thus, whatever He does is just, even if we do not understand it. When we do not understand, our response should be to appeal directly to God, not a law of fairness according to us. For we trust God for Who He is in addition to what He does.

Job professes, "He's killing me, yet will I serve Him." We will all have this moment in some form. This moment of choice.

When we suffer, not knowing or believing the Word of God, we can fail to develop and digest the lessons and strength we were meant to receive through the Spirit of God.

*Blessed is the man who perseveres under trial, because when he has stood the test, he will receive the crown of life that God has promised to those who love him* (James 1:12).

God knows He can take us to other places in Himself. As He prepares us for that place, there is often turbulence. But turbulence is employed to cultivate us on the way to that other place and rightly prepare us for the assignment or blessing. What we know now will aid us through our storm, but it is not sufficient for the next level. Going through our storm will strengthen us, expand our knowledge, increase our wisdom, and fortify our understanding of the hidden things of God to be revealed that will sustain us on the next level.

From chapters four through chapter 37, Job and his friends go back and forth over right and wrong and what's on God's mind. They thought they were arguing God's point. After all, there had to be a reason for so much tragedy in one person's life. Surely God takes care of His own. Certainly it is the wicked that suffer consequences, and we as children of God walk on the clouds above the fray. No evil should touch us.

Job was thrown into the pile of all of those that deserve what happens to them. One enlightened friend after another threw him to the wolves, and Job was devoured by the words of his friends instead of uplifted by them. They told him over and over how he needed to repent and do this and do that to get back in with God and stop calling God on the carpet because, according to them, Job must have needed to be punished.

It is easy for others to write off those who are going through trouble. It is easy to walk away, and it is easy to rationalize that somehow it is the consequence of who or what they are, never realizing that maybe something other than what we see is in play. That is the difference between the mind of man and the mind of God.

Yes, we will all suffer the consequences of our actions, but when trouble is not a consequence of our actions and something is coming against us, try to be mindful of where God is in our situation. Do not let others condemn you and please do not condemn yourself. It will stunt your growth and delay what God is doing. God trusts you enough with a storm that will bring Him glory and bring you great reward.

Like I said before, many times I played the reel of my past life to see what was so egregious that God saw fit for this punishment. Why was it that when I did what others have done or less than they have, I am dealt *this* hand and they walk with no cares of this life? But again, that is a spirit of confusion and distortion. There's no reason to stay in the desert forty years when we know that we can get to our Promised Land in a few short days if we trust God's Word to us.

It is stated by experts that there are seven stages of grief:

✓ **Shock and Denial** in which we are numbed in our disbelief that this could even happen.

✓ **Pain and Guilt**. When the shock begins to wear off, the pain settles in and can often be overwhelming. The excruciating and almost unbearable pain makes you desire and crave any release, whether it is alcohol, drugs, or even death. The guilt is often associated with what we have lost within our loss. For me, I lost a future when Madison passed. In this stage, we often have guilt for not doing what we wanted to do or could have done to prevent loss; or guilt because we assume we had a power that we did not, that we believed could or should have been able to prevent the situation.

✓ **Anger and Bargaining** is where we lash out and lay unwarranted blame, even on God, Who we trusted would relieve us from the inevitable. Like Job, we go through the "Why me?"

✓ **Depression, Reflection, and Loneliness** if we believe that God has abandoned us. Job's friends wanted him not to feel alone and wanted to lift him out of his depression; but with Job verbalizing his feelings in his depression and reflecting over his life, they felt it necessary to get him straight and move him into agreement with their understanding, not because it was right, but because they wanted to feel like what they saw could not happen to them because they were not like him and knew better than him. It is important for us to go through this phase and dredge out the filth that confusion and a too-soon separation lay waste. We should express what we feel even if what we think it is not based on truth, just to exercise it out of us. The spirit of truth will always prevail. Once we deal with how we feel and connect it with what we know to be true, eventually we get to a point of realization and achieve what they call the stage of

✓ **Turnaround**. This fosters reconstruction. I call this transformation of the mind. Once we transform our mind, we can begin to test the knowledge of the new mind. This transformation is ushered in by searching the Word for truth to ease our suffering mind and heart. Laying hold to the promise and the rhema word. We want things to make sense to us. With a clear mind despite our emotions, we find that clarity and peace in the midst of the storm. That quiet whisper where God speaks. Going through this will usher in the

✓ **Reconstruction and Working Through**, the energy to deal with the real issues, learning that there are things that only time can heal, and this is one of them.

✓ **Acceptance and Hope**. When we accept the truth of our situation and who God is in our lives, we can walk with a full understanding of God's will and trust that all things work out for our good. We become free to let Him drive us, and we release the wheel. We travail, and believe that what we birth will bring about more joy than our current sorrow.

Not everyone goes through all seven stages of grief, but we do know there is a conversation with one's self in which we comb through our library of life to figure out how this situation fits as a consequence of who we are. When people do this, our job is not to rake them over the coals, but support them where they are, as Jesus did with Peter.

My father always states that we must ask ourselves when we are told things, why are we being told what we are being told, who is telling us this information, and what benefit do they get from what they are telling us. We know that Job's friends did love him and had the best of intentions, but we also know that they were frustrated with Job's inability to humble himself and accept his fate due to his sin—according to them—not because what they were saying was right. The truth is Job's friends were concerned that if Job was not sinful and suffered this, what did that mean for them? He could not be right and suffer because that would make them vulnerable; they did not want to accept that as truth because that would mean it could happen to them as well.

Job was steadfast because he knew better. Job's unwillingness to accept their "wisdom" moved his friends from a place of comfort to a place of reproach.

When Chris and I did not act according to how many felt we should through our ordeal and did not grieve in the way they believed we should, we were branded as being in denial, close to a nervous breakdown, wearing a mask, and so on. People were pushing counseling of every kind from family, loss/grief, to marriage because of what someone else went through or because of what someone else said. When we said "no thanks, we are okay," they were offended—like *how dare we think we can do it on our own, others could not, who do we think we are?* There was one opinion after another on how we should act, what we should do, why Chris shouldn't be at work, what I should do, and where I should be when he was at work. It was the weirdest thing. Then there were those folks that actually sat around waiting for us to fall apart. We heard so many rumors. Even the well-meaning individuals sometimes did not understand that we were okay.

We had each other, and we had our faith. People, even Christians, did not get that. They thought it was a line we were handing out and we were some kind of freaks blowing off getting better. We understood that we were in this together and we had it under control. Yes, it hurt. Yes, we were in a world alone. Yes, we had a million questions for God and had a lot to go through in ourselves and contemplating our future. But because we would not conform to others' ideas of what should happen, we became the problem; something was wrong with us because we did not accept or do things the way others thought. People can be unbelievable.

In the text, God addresses Job directly and answers all of Job's questions and puts everything he has gone through into perspective. Job admits that he only knew of God, but not until his loss and suffering, did he come to know God intimately. Job admits in chapter 42: *"I heard about you before, but now I have seen you with my own eyes. I take back everything I said, and I sit in dust and ashes to show my repentance."*

Sometimes it is the worst places in our lives where we meet God face-to-face.

Job realized that, though he was right about what he knew about God, he did not have the full understanding that comes through knowing God in relationship, not in ceremony, tradition, or religion. His mind had been transformed, and he was able to accept and understand the sovereignty of God. There is no one above the law or too righteous for God to transform or for the enemy to come against.

What is an even greater point to remember in this text is that God says that Job is correct in his knowledge of the mode of operation of God; he just thought too much of himself in relation with God and lacked full understanding. But he also states how wrong Job's friends were. This negates the accusatory notion often associated with affliction and supported by verse from the book of Job. We find that though Job's friends were correctly recorded in the book of Job, all of what they said was not correct in context and therefore we shouldn't allow others to continue to use the book of Job to persecute those that endure. We should look to God's Word for direction in helping us heal and, in turn, aiding others in fulfilling God's promise and healing in their lives.

The very people who were condemning Job were now instructed to give an offering and be prayed for by Job (Job 42:7–8). The tables turned, as they often do. God accepted Job's prayer on their behalf. We should be careful who and how we rebuke anyone.

*"Do not judge, and you will not be judged. Do not condemn, and you will not be condemned. Forgive, and you will be forgiven. Give, and it will be given to you. A good measure, pressed down, shaken together and running over, will be poured into your lap. For with the measure you use, it will be measured to you"* (Luke 6:37).

Elihu was right when he said that God uses suffering to teach, discipline, and refine us, but there is still more to this; it is about trusting and leaning on God because He is God. We must be careful of what we accept in our spirits as the truth of Who God is, because if we accept the wrong things—things not based solely on God's Word—God will appear to be contradictory in His ways, and we will not be able to accept or grow in what He has for us. We will get stuck in our pain. God uses suffering, but God doesn't cause the suffering.

Discernment and prayer should always be accompanied with the reading of the Word and studying of the Word because one person's interpretation of the Word may not be what God is speaking in our situation. What is God saying to you? What has been purposed for the fulfillment of your destiny? We know what the written word says, but what has God said directly to you?

What is your "Rhema" word for your life, for your situation? It will echo from the Scripture. The Scripture is your hope; the spoken word is your faith substance. Is He telling you to be still—He will fight the battle, or is He telling you to go out and fight, and He will deliver the victory into your hands? They are both scripturally correct, but what did God tell you was for you?

God was telling me that it would be all right. He kept showing me in dreams that Madison would receive perfect healing. I saw her in white, healed and perfect in every way. He would show me two little girls and one looked just like Madison. He showed me so much, and there was a peace at the end of each dream, so I believed that meant she would live and be healed. I held on to what God did for others and the wisdom many encouraged me with scripturally. I held on to his written word and what God did for many in the Bible, but the only thing that mattered was what God actually said.

He never told me she would live. He never told me He would take away the cancer. He told me I would be all right. He told me she would be all right and would receive perfection, that there would be perfect healing. He told me He was with me. In my mind, I took that to mean what I wanted it to mean. Perfect healing—what could be more perfect than being with the Lord never to deal with this issue again; He perfectly healed during this. We both were perfected. In the end He did tell me that the healing was meant for me. I was healed, made free. The number 3 was on Madison's clothing in the dream. The number 3 represents divine perfection and completion. She was perfected and healed. She received her reward for the work she did in my life. She had no worries anymore. I am all right and restored. He took care of me even when I did not want Him to, and He perfected me in Him.

I often had dreams of standing with little girls in my future. I thought at least one of them was Madison. They looked so much like her. The little girls were actually the twins with which I was pregnant the month after Madison died. Everything God had showed me came to pass. Everything He told me was true. He showed me everything I needed to know, but I could not see clearly. I could not understand.

*Then He came to Bethsaida; and they brought a blind man to Him, and begged Him to touch him. So He took the blind man by the hand and led him out of the town. And when He had spit on his eyes and put His hands on him, He asked him if he saw anything. And he looked up and said, "I see men like trees, walking." Then He put His hands on his eyes again and made him look up. And he was restored and saw everyone clearly* (Mark 8:22–25).

In reading His Word and standing strong in faith, His voice comforted me. The visions God sent were in response to prayer, yet I was holding on to what I thought. I was interpreting unto my desire and not looking at what God was really showing me. He was showing me truth; He was showing me His faithfulness, His restoring power. Encouraging me to stay in faith, to persevere no matter what. It changed my life and I know I can do anything through Christ. I can withstand all things through Christ. My vision changed – I see the blessing in things.

We must, no matter what, even when God doesn't give us what we want at that moment, even if He doesn't respond in the way we want at the moment we desire, continue serving and trusting Him because He is God. A delay is not always denial. We can accept whatever the outcome because we realize that it is a part of the path already prescribed for us before we were ever created or in our mother's womb and it will work out for our good. God is not a contradiction, nor does He lie.

## Chapter Twelve

# *Perseverance*

*He sent from above, He took me; He drew me out of many waters. He delivered me from my strong enemy...But the Lord was my support. He also brought me out into a broad place; He delivered me because He delighted in me. The Lord rewarded me according to my righteousness.... The Lord lives! Blessed be my Rock! Let the God of my salvation be exalted (Psalm 18:13–46).*

SOMETIMES I WOULD GO IN my living room, lay on the sofa and just cry. I would cry so loud and so hard I would put myself to sleep. The pain was so intense. It felt like my soul was ripped out and I was a half functioning empty vessel. The screams of my void, my hollowness, was deafening. I would internalize the story of Job. I would visualize myself walking in his victory. That God would find me not guilty as well and I would receive my reward. I would feel his restoration as my restoration. I would imagine switching my mourning for joy and praise for my heaviness. My spirit would leave my body on that sofa or in the bed and I would witness my spirit, my strength standing before me, preaching to me and encouraging me. I was my own audience.

If my writing is sometimes a little preachy it is because that is how I made it through. I would visualize myself standing as a preaching minister. I was my own prophet bringing forth a Word from the Lord to my spirit. The accounts of the Bible quickened my spirit. I was lifted up from my low place with truth.

As I spoke, I would see the room fill with others in need of hearing my words, needing to hear my story. My story was the foundation of the text in which the word became truth and the promise of the Word manifested.

I did this because I had to keep going, I told myself. "Someone needs me to keep going. I need me to keep going. God needs me to keep going so I can get what's mine. I will not die here. I will not give up"

Madison finished her race and completed her mission. I had to do the same. It was hard to accept that she had to die or that she was a force to usher me into my purpose. She was my baby—not the ushering force on my path—she was my baby. No one wants to believe their baby is the angel to help them walk into their anointing and that in their baby's death they themselves will receive life. What kind of life is that?

I just wanted her to be my child, not to save me, but just as she accepted her purpose, I would eventually accept it, too. I would eventually accept it all and go back over it for it to make sense and for me to realize the blessing in disguise. It was important to do. If I failed, if I fell apart, then her life, her purpose, her sacrifice would be in vain. I refused to allow that. She meant the world to me. Just like I will not fail God, I will not fail her. She was my giver of life.

God's ways are a mystery, but in the end, when we are not so attached to what He is touching, we can understand them. They make sense in the scheme of the larger picture. We want our prayers to change things, and they do. We want to hold out hope for our hearts' desire, because it works, but we must also accept what has been put before us. We shouldn't try to avoid what will make us stronger. We shouldn't avoid our wilderness because it will prepare us for our Promised Land.

We must remember that it is not all about us in particular, but inclusively. I encouraged myself to never stop, never give up. I knew perseverance was the only way to receive my reward. I knew perseverance would bring glory to God and reward Madison for a job well done.

I prayed, I studied, I listened to hours of the Word and I cried through it because at times when I was conscious of my situation, the natural self would say, *Why are you pressing through? You thought you had it right before, you thought you knew it was true before and look where you are.* But I had no other choice. The alternative was not for me to accept. So I kept reading and searching for more understanding, encouragement and the echo that said I was on the right path. I knew I could not be in a delusion, God was real, I was real, and His voice and word were real. I needed to know I was alright and ensure myself to hold on because it was not over, this was not the end. I refused to let it be.

God showed me that I am because God *is*, and others will become because I am. I was instructed to write and persevere and record what I did and how I got over.

*Now, go, write it before them on a tablet and inscribe it in a book, that it may be as a witness for the time to come forevermore* (Isaiah 30:8).

I am not in this alone, nor are the things any of us go through for or about us alone. We are the Body of Christ; we are the church in which God abides. There are works to be performed, developed, and nurtured that minister and bless the world, not the church made by man's hand. That church should only be your Home Depot, aiding you in the constant renovation and enlarging that happens within us.

Let us accept the cup that is given to us and believe what God has already told us—that it will be all right. No matter what, He is here with us. No matter what, He will work it out for our good.

*"Perseverance must finish its work so that you may be mature and complete, not lacking anything"* (James 1:4).

James goes on to say that we are blessed when we endure the trial, because after the test, we receive the crown of life that God has promised to those who love Him (James 1:12).

If we persevere in our endeavors, not just by staying strong against the winds of life, but by humbling ourselves before the throne and allowing God to use the moment of distress to form us into our intended creation, we will have all that we desire and God will make us more than we could have expected of ourselves and give us life abundantly.

It is true that the sufferings of our present time do not compare to the glory that will soon be revealed in us through overcoming, perseverance, and opening of our spirit. The opening of our spirit to God allows us to receive understanding of the wisdom we have been granted through our difficulty. There are a lot of people who can read the Word of God and quote its words, but lack insight into its depth and purpose in their lives because the truths have not been exercised in their lives - especially in difficult times.

In this time, I found that in my weakest moments, God *is* strongest. I allowed Him in this moment of surrender to press His secret spiritual understanding upon me in my empty yet accepting state. I learned that when I am broken in the midst of the wilderness, and nothing makes sense, when I stop to gather myself in silence waiting for direction, a word, something, or anything to give me a sign that will lead me out of this place, he speaks.

During these moments of revelation, all the clouds of my mind are pushed aside, and I stretch my mind, vision, and ears toward Him in order to focus and receive the larger picture God has painted.

I clear my slate for a Word from God to be written on my being that will lead me where I need to go. Not just any word, but the Word from God that is for me and me alone in my situation.

At the beginning of my trial, I thought I knew God and His mode of operation. I thought I knew myself. Not until I was in the middle of the trial did I realize everything that I knew, I had heard and absorbed from and for others. These interpretations of the Word were not wrong, but they were not singing my song. I needed to receive a Word for *me*. I needed to hear the song written for *me* to sing and have it written upon my heart.

I could no longer dance to the beat of religion and general spiritual understanding accepted and hoped on by others, by most everyone. The hope of His Word may have worked for me up until then, but when hell showed up at my door I needed to receive direction for me that was according to the will and purpose of God established for *me* based in His Word, but spoken in accordance to the will He established for me.

That could only come by way of relationship with God, not vicariously.

I needed to be in relationship with Him who created me and had spoken my destiny before time began. I needed to contact that voice that was recorded upon my spirit to hear what God was playing for and saying to me. I realized that once I knew Him, I would also know me. Once I began to seek his kingdom first, everything else would be added unto me. So I pressed on.

## Chapter Thirteen

# *The Glory of the Lord Is Risen Upon Me*

*"Before I formed you in the womb I knew you, before you were born I set you apart; I appointed you as a prophet to the nations." "Ah, Sovereign LORD," I said, "I do not know how to speak; I am only a child." But the LORD said to me, "Do not say, 'I am only a child.' You must go to everyone I send you to and say whatever I command you. Do not be afraid of them, for I am with you and will rescue you," declared the LORD. Then the LORD reached out his hand and touched my mouth and said to me, "Now, I have put my words in your mouth. See, today I appoint you over nations and kingdoms to uproot and tear down, to destroy and overthrow, to build and to plan" (Jeremiah 1:5).*

BEFORE WE CAME TO THIS planet, God set us aside for His purpose. He established our life and the journey that would aid us in completing that purpose. Before we entered the womb, God whispered our assignment to us. It was not based on the ideals and abilities society deemed necessary for us to be great-it was what God said about us that made us the right person, the one in whom greatness abides to bring forth life and revelation into the lives of others through our testimony at the appointed time.

We are commissioned to do certain things and learn certain lessons, heal certain hurts and overcome certain obstacles as we build our most holy faith to walk in Him and die having fulfilled our mission. Madison died when she fulfilled her mission. She did in thirteen months what some of us cannot do in eighty years. She saved me and led me into a purpose established for me. Not just me, but many others.

After she passed, my sister-in-law called us to check out the online responses to Madison's obituary on the newspaper's Web site. There were so many people I did not know and never heard of that heard Madison's story. There were encouraging notes and messages from many stating how Madison's story helped them through their ordeals. That our faith and determination that was told to them from nurses, hospital staff, church members, and friends who assisted them through things they were going through at that time in their lives. That Chris's and my ability to stay together and stay strong even after her passing spoke to them, and through our story they were encouraging others that had suffered loss. That through the courage of Madison, through the stories of her never being down a day in her life, they gained hope. Her smile always lighting up a room. Her tiny voice filling everyone's spirit that came in contact with her, her ability to endure to the end was encouraging. Many cancer patients and family members of cancer patients spoke of the encouragement it gave them.

If little Madison could endure and if Chris and I could have faith no matter what came, they believed they could as well. It was heartwarming. It was always something about her that drew people, and none of us could explain it until my angel ascended to her rightful place of reward.

People were watching us and we did not know it. Someone needed an example of a fighter. Someone wanted to see strength in a storm and they saw it in us. That was amazing to me. Someone is watching you for leadership, service, love, kindness, victory, success, direction. There is a child, a friend, a family member, a coworker, or even a stranger that is looking to you to lead them in their walk. You can lead them to life or defeat with your choices. Someone is waiting for you to win. Someone is waiting for you to be courageous and to fight the good fight. You give them the okay to walk the path that you yourself have traveled—where will that path lead?

God showed me how important I am to the process of life. He showed me why Jesus is so important to us. Because He is our example and we are to be a representation of Him in the earth. To be like Him meant I had to walk in His ability, walk upright and accept my cup and win. God has called me to win and causes me to triumph in all things. Through the power of Jesus Christ I can and I will.

All that I have, all that I have been allowed to go through is about overcoming for others. We may be overcoming for those that came before us, destroying strongholds and repairing brokenness inherited by us, so that we can bring victory to those that will come after us, so they will not have to deal with the iniquities and destruction of a past they did not live, but was inflicted upon them.

Our lives are meant to help repair the world one spirit at a time. When we heal, the world heals. When we win, the world wins. We are that important to the progression of life and the kingdom of God.

When you choose death, you breed death, when you choose life, you open the windows of heaven upon yourself and those around you. We must go through our circumstances and be victorious so that we are a testament to someone else. We are the blessing we are looking for. When I bless someone else, I get free. Everything you want for you, if you give it to someone else -that which you did not think you had will appear. Once you awaken it, the overflow of abundance of life shows bright, and you will keep on giving and transforming. Everything will become clear and the journey and its happenings will start to make sense.

On my walk, there is someone that I must encourage to overcome because they have to help someone else, and so on. We all must accomplish the things set before us so that everyone around us can do the same. If not, others waiting for us to be free will be delayed in their own freedom. They are waiting for us to shine as the example of "yes, you can make it."

Madison was not only a blessing to me; she was a blessing to others because her coming, her loving, her death, and her resurrection with Christ is a testament that this thing, this faith walk, this purposeful existence is real. If one part of the Word of God is real, you can believe the rest to be true. You can trust it and try it for yourself.

This life is about us in connection with our beginning power. I had to try it to trust it and trust it to try it. Let me encourage you to *try it*! Trust me on this. Every principle established by God is unfailing. His word is unfathomable. Start using your faith in small things to strengthen your faith muscles to prepare you to walk through big things. You will be all that you desired, but never knew how to be.

We must open ourselves to the message that was written on our spirit and echoes in the written Word, that we are to bring forth life to those around us through the Spirit of God and His truth that abides in us. It is granted to us for our journey, the power to overcome. We have a message. We all have a message, have power, have importance. The world and the cares of this world have clouded judgment and confused signals from the Lord. Instead of using the lessons of our trials to better lives and encourage others, we allow them to shame us.

Whatever your loss is or was—children, innocence through molestation, physical abuse, sexual abuse, a job, a home, a ministry, a marriage—loss is loss, but let's realize there is purpose in all of us— even in all loss—and we are all a testimony. What is your testament to the truth of life?

There is nothing shameful about our stories, because they do not define us, they only tell us how far we have come and how strong we are because we endured. The gap of our journey from there to here is not shameful, it is victorious. It shows the God factor in our life. We are a blessing to someone waiting to happen.

After knowing this, the question is, *will we choose to walk in our purpose?* It is a choice - no one can make us do it, no one can make us love God, no one can make us pray. Not even God goes against our will. This is all about choice. Will we pick up our broken body and continue on, knowing that though we may be battered and scared and may carry the evidence of our lowest and heaviest moments, we *will* be free of the burden by walking toward our destiny?

Trust that the Word of God will heal us. Believe that the old will fall off and newness will be put on. These dry bones can and were created to have new life. The resurrection power that was in Jesus Christ is also in us. God gives the power to heal our lives, our relationships, our brokenness, our emptiness, and everything else. Do we trust Him?

Do we have the will to try again? Will we be like Eve and trust the promise that the seed is within through Christ? When our lives seem contrary to truth, do we have the strength to try again? To move ahead and reach for what we have been promised is ours? Do you believe, though your Cain and Abel are no longer here and it looks like things are worse when you were told they would be better, that the promise is true and not the current circumstance? That the circumstance is not your end? That you can begin again, conceive again, and receive your Seth? That your promise may not come through the first try, but if you have a promise from God, it will come to pass? You just cannot give up-you have to try again. Keep on pushing and never give up. Do you believe that the pain doesn't outweigh the rewards?

I talk about my trial to many, and in those times, when I am most vulnerable to my pain, others are released of their shame to share their own stories. They feel okay to share because I am okay with my imperfection, allowing them to embrace theirs.

I realize that a lot of us hold shame for what we have gone through, for our doubt, for not receiving what we thought would be our victory even though we stood strong in faith, for our imperfections, for failures and missteps, for lack of knowledge, and for a whole host of other reasons. I want to tell you, don't ever feel ashamed of your story.

If the wicked are not ashamed of their crimes, why are we ashamed of our growth? When we know better, we do better. But God has also shown us in the story of the potter that just because we have been marred in this life doesn't negate who God has already predestined us to be.

In Jeremiah 18, the potter did not change the clay he was working with because it was marred. Instead, he continued to work with it in its state and transformed it into something even more beautiful and unique and suitable than it would have been before it was scarred. There is nothing more unique or more valuable than a perfect creation with hints of naturally occurring imperfections that are beautified by its creator. The same applies to us. Our imperfections make us more valuable, not less.

I remember right after Madison passed, I continued to have a lot of dreams. I could not wait to go to sleep; there was comfort in my dreams. Then I had no dreams for a few days. During this time I spent my days and nights in prayer, crying and reading the Word. God directed me to do some things – prayer for individuals, situations, forgiveness, etc, and I did them despite what I felt like doing. God restored Job when he prayed for his friends (Job 42:10). Then I had another dream.

I dreamed I awoke in my bed and noticed that the dining room in my house was lit up. The light was not on, but the room was illuminated. Chris and I got out of the bed and went to see why it was so bright. I thought Madison had come to visit me again. I was walking in anticipation. When we left the room and walked into the living room, an evergreen tree, a Christmas tree, appeared in the middle of the room. It was huge, about fifteen feet tall. The tip was all the way up to the ceiling.

After it fully appeared, lights and decorations began forming on the tree, like a beautiful Christmas tree. The room was gorgeous, and the lights on the tree made the room even brighter. There were wrapped gifts under the tree and piled up in the hall between the living room and the hall near the front door. All of the gifts were wrapped in shiny red, gold and white wrapping paper.

The first thing that caught my eye among all the gifts was a lavish diamond ring. The top of the box was closed, but it had a virtual picture on the outside of it that depicted the ring inside. On the picture of the gift, my mother's name was written. She was in the back room and heard us in the dining room. She came in the dining room while I was admiring the ring, and she said, "Oh, my God, that is the ring we looked at the other day. It is exactly what I wanted."

I replied, "I know—how did she get that for you?" We were bewildered. We assumed that Madison and God had done something, but we did not understand what was going on. The ring was triangular, with three ornate gold lines—one on each side, and the middle was filled with rows of ¼-carat diamonds.

All the other gifts we assumed were Madison's or were in connection with Madison, but we waited in anticipation to see if something else was about to happen that would make this make sense. I looked at the gifts before us, and there were numbers on them. The same number with different letters in my mother's handwriting. She looked at it and asked out loud to no one in particular, "How did they do this? I wanted to give this to her." She went back to the back room to get my father.

Chris and I were standing there trying to figure out what was going on and what it all meant. Then the room went back to its usual state. We started talking again, and the room lit up again, the tree reappeared, the lights on the tree reappeared, and the room was even brighter than before. All of a sudden, two women came from around the corner of the hallway with gifts. We noticed there was a line of women behind them, all standing two by two all the way down the hall. We accepted the gifts and said thank you. As they walked away, I asked Chris who they were. He said their names, but I did not recognize any of them. Chris knew everyone.

The main focus for my point is the gifts. At the time, it did not make sense. But a few months later, it made a lot of sense. My mother took my daughter's passing very hard. On the way to the funeral, my mother got a vision of only one word: *restored.* She wrote the word across the entire page of her journal while on the plane and closed the book. When I called her about a month or so later and told her I was pregnant, she was elated and told me about her vision and what she wrote. She said she did not know what exactly it meant when it was shown to her, but now she did.

The gift, the ring for her, was from God. The gifts for Chris and me that had her handwriting on them were her desires for us and our prayers being answered in multiplication. The gifts with the numbers on them, I would later find, were my twin daughters. Gifts from God. The numbers on the gifts were the same numbers the doctor assigned them to differentiate the twins during the ultrasound. The doctor did not know, but God gave me a sign in that dream and I held on to it even though I did not understand.

When I received the full revelation of the dream, I knew there was nothing to worry about during that pregnancy. I was carrying gifts of restoration, and nothing can take away God's gifts—they are forever. What excited me even more was that the room was filled with gifts I never opened, and even more gifts were being brought to us by the line of women in the hall. I was excited to see what God had in store.

I was pregnant with twin girls. My mother got what she wanted, and Chris and I got what we wanted. It was already done before it came into the earth.

I remember about eight or ten weeks into the pregnancy, I had another dream. A demon came into my room at the end of my bed, and I began to plead the blood of Jesus. I began to speak against him, and he shook and trembled until he disappeared. I awoke and had another dream. I dreamed that I had to go to the bathroom; and when I went in, a demon came into the bathroom, and I stood up and began to speak against him. I lifted up my hand and told him that he would be the last one to ever come in here. I was sick of them, I was not scared of them, and I would never lose to them. I opened my fist, and as if he was in the palm of my hand, I wrenched my fist closed and crushed him into a ball. I threw him in the toilet and flushed.

I woke up and really had to go to the bathroom. When I went, I passed a mass the size of a fist and I bled. I remember screaming when I saw the blood. Chris ran into the bathroom shaken, with fear on his face, not looking forward to any more drama. I got myself together as soon as I saw his face. The Holy Spirit spoke to me. I remember hearing over and over, "fear doesn't live here anymore."

The dream of the evergreen tree came to me, and I began to speak into my situation. I knew what God said, what He showed me, and what His Word said. I was confident and not confused. I knew exactly what He said, and there was no illusion or self imaginations. I had the power and faith. I had the spoken Word, a vision, and the confirmation of the Holy Spirit at this moment; I had no reason to fear. The Lord's voice is all the power and authority I needed. I was not going backward. If I could believe with a Word as general as "you will be all right," I could believe with a more concrete Word of "I will restore you, and here is your reward."

I said out loud to Chris a summary that played in my spirit and in my head, and he walked in agreement with me. We both decided to go to bed; we were not worried or concerned. We would go to our doctor's appointment the next day as planned, not the emergency room. We would not be moved. Everything was fine; it was one of those things that occurred during early pregnancy. I felt peace, and we went to bed.

Sure enough, when we went to the doctor, there was no problem; it was just one of those flukes that sometimes happen when you get pregnant. I went full-term with my pregnancy with no problems. The doctors could not believe it. All of their other multiple pregnancies were on bed rest, in the hospital, or having some other issue. I had not one issue, and both girls were full-term and healthy. I trusted, and He did His part.

The girls looked so much like Madison when they were born that I had to stop myself from believing that God had answered my prayer and sent her back in a new body. It might not be her in either of my twins, but the same energy, joy and sweet spirit are present. On top of that, the baby the angel showed me, I had her. She is one of the twins.

The two little girls in my dream that were being taught before their birthing in the upper room, I had them. They look the same, one with curly hair and one with straight hair, one a little thicker than the other. Though they both look a lot like Madison, one looks just like Madison. Even her baby pictures are exactly like Madison's in look and in pose. I was restored.

So many of us are looking for wholeness, looking for purpose—who we are and what our part in this world is. Wondering how we overcome and be the greatness we were created to be? The answer is that you will find your purpose in your problems. Solve and overcome your problems, your iniquities, your generational curses, your affliction, and you will find your testimony and your purpose.

You will have an answer for someone behind you walking that path you once walked. Give them the directions that assisted you out of your situation. Heal your land in order to help someone else heal theirs. We cannot take anyone to a place we have not been. We cannot tell anyone about a journey or a place we have not gone or experienced, do not trust, do not believe in, or have not lived out. It is one thing to know about something - it is another thing to have been there and done that. We that have been there can tell others about things that someone who just knows, but has not experienced, has no idea about.

Purpose is fulfilled every day. In all of our issues, in our daily dealings with people, we fulfill purpose. We sow seeds of life or death. There shouldn't be one purpose we strive to fulfill. There are many purposes we will meet in this life. But we will not fulfill that major purpose we are all seeking to achieve if we do not fulfill the daily purposes in our lives. God will not take you to a place or give you what you are not first prepared to receive. You must make a habit of completing daily purpose and being a blessing in small things. Then your assignment will grow to be greater and more impactful. You will fulfill your desire.

If you cannot heal the land in your own heart or in your own home, how can you help heal someone else's? You have no record of success. Unless you will be the story of defeat— and who wants to be that kind of messed-up example? Be an example of triumph, not the person everyone should learn how not to be.

Jesus came for the Jews first, then the Gentiles. He came to heal and bring salvation and restoration to us all, but He started with Himself first. Once He was baptized naturally and spiritually and verified by the Father, he entered into His ministry, His mission and fulfilled His purpose. Then he went out and drew near the disciples, the Jewish people, the Gentiles, and now the world believes. But we must start with self first. We must allow God to heal our family and our relationships before we try to conquer the world.

When we fulfill our purpose, it impacts today and tomorrow. My grandparents and great-grandparents fulfilled purpose because they not only impacted their generations and family at the time of their lives, but they have also impacted me. I live under the covenants and promises established through their obedience and love walk with God. God gives us that which He has sworn to our forefathers as well as what He has promised us directly.

Every day I ask myself what have I done today on my love walk that impacts generations to come? What strongholds have I created or defeated? What legacy have I left in the spirit of my lineage to deal with or rejoice in? Will the blessing or curse be upon my children and descendents? What power will awaken in them? A power of greatness urging a walk with God—or a power of defeat, addiction, low self-esteem, or depression?

*Behold, I set before you today a blessing and a curse: the blessing, if you obey the commandments of the LORD your God which I command you today; and the curse, if you do not obey the commandments of the LORD your God, but turn aside from the way which I command you today, to go after other gods which you have not known* (Deut. 11: 26–28).

I no longer carry my trial as a burden. The pain and the emptiness of Madison not being here and the feeling of being helpless in my efforts still cause my heart and soul sadness, and I still cry sometimes like it just happened yesterday. However, I realize that this earthly trip is not about me. I take nothing personally. I only try to do my part.

My suffering is only one chapter of the entire book of my life. This hurt is the worst I will ever experience in my book, but I understand bad things happen to all people, not just me. And because of my faith, because I know who my God is and who I am in Him, my reward is great. I declare that and receive that!

I choose to believe the Word God has spoken over my life. I believe that He has nothing but good planned for me despite what comes against me.

*"For I know the plans I have for you," declares the LORD, "plans to prosper you and not to harm you, plans to give you hope and a future"* (Jeremiah 29:11).

God has spoken a Word over all of us that is power to sustain us through everything in our life that seeks to break us down. It keeps us held up above all circumstances and moves us forward toward our destiny, even when we feel like giving up. It is that Voice, that I AM that declares in you, *no, this is not your place to die. This is your place of pain, yes, your place of repositioning, your place of preparation, but not your place of dying.* That is why no weapon formed against us will ever prosper. We are more than conquerors. We are highly favored, walking in the power and authority afforded us by the sacrifice and resurrection of Jesus Christ. We are redeemed!

It may get hard at times, and we may want the mountain moved. We have the power to speak to the mountain, so why not move it? But sometimes the mountain is necessary.

The Apostle Paul, who is responsible for most of the epistles of the New Testament, went through the same thing.

*To keep me from becoming conceited because of these surpassingly great revelations, there was given me a thorn in my flesh, a messenger of Satan, to torment me. Three times I pleaded with the Lord to take it away from me. But he said to me, "My grace is sufficient for you, for my power is made perfect in weakness." Therefore I will boast all the more gladly about my weaknesses, so that Christ's power may rest on me. That is why, for Christ's sake, I delight in weaknesses, in insults, in hardships, in persecutions, in difficulties. For when I am weak, then I am strong* (2 Corinthians 12:7–10).

We may have some hills to climb, but we have the power of Christ to triumph over everything. Let God be true and every negative circumstance be a lie. If we have invited Christ into our hearts as Lord and Savior, we possess all of His being. We, through His power - His Spirit, can call things that are not as though they were, and they shall be according to His will. No matter how unique we are, we all have the same measure of faith to be activated in our lives and in our situations.

And we can be confident that this place of hurt, shame, lack, whatever it is for you, we shall never return again. When God restores you, just like Job, you no longer have to live in fear, but go forward in power. After I lost Madison, I told Chris, "there is nothing that can happen to me that will cause me to move. I have no fear and know I will always be all right. If I can lose my child and still have my mind and be here functioning, there is nothing man can do to me or say to me that can move me out of where God has set me. I have felt the worst hurt a mother could feel, and no one but God was able to comfort me. If God be for me, He is more than the world against me. He kept me and restored me. I know His Word is true.

I know who I trust in, Who abides in me; and no one can do anything to me. Even death has no sting anymore." Do not allow the clouds of yesterday to hover over your today. The enemy wants you to hold onto your disappointments in hopes that you will block your own progress, walking in a spirit of turmoil and discontent—but who is made free, is free indeed.

Job never lacked or lost again after he was restored. He was restored, raised higher, and further prospered at every hand, and until the day he died, he won. He went through the test. God kept him and restored him according to His will, His riches and glory.

When something has been allowed to be taken from you, as a child of God, you have to know in your heart, mind, and spirit that He will replace it with something new. You can trust that you will put on the garment of praise for your spirit of heaviness and the oil of joy for your mourning.

Accept and enjoy the Promised Land you have been led into, eat from its fruit, and partake in its flowing of milk and honey.

When you reach your destination, make sure you tell your story. It is a unique and important story. Just as you are unique, your story is unique. There is no one with a story like yours. There may be similar stories, but your story is original, because you are original to the story. My story is not better or worse than the next person's. What makes mine great is that I am a unique creation in the story, and my awareness of God's presence and transformation of me into what He wanted to create makes my story worth telling for someone else's deliverance and perseverance.

God is great for so many reasons. But one is definitely because He loves His creation, no matter how marred the clay. It is His, and that is all He cares about, loving His creation. He sees what *He* created and not what man damaged. No matter what you go through, know that God's plan and purpose for you has not changed, but has become even more important as you, His creation, learns your importance to the greater plan of God in this life.

I was told to write more about me in my own words when I wrote this book and less of the Word of God. But I could not leave out the Word of God. God's Words are my word and my words are God's Words. I could say that I did not want to preach to anyone, but this is how it was received by me. Through the word. It was neither through a single revelation nor from the Holy Spirit and I having a onetime moment. It was through dedication and relationship to His Word that I received the spoken word, revelation and restoration in my spirit. I believed before I received. I heard before I believed, and I read before I heard.

His word kept me, strengthened me, showed me who I was and where I was going. Many people think the Bible is a book of characters and historical events where God was referenced. A genealogy of a man named Jesus. It is not a genealogy of priest and believers of God. It is not. It is not about historical characters and the events in their lives. It is a book about us. It shows us who we are and it illustrates the events of our lives and circumstances already played out. It is not about anyone, but us. We see who we are and where we are going through the Bible, the Word of God.

When I read the stories and write about Job and everyone else it is because through them God showed me who I was. He showed me - me. He showed me my victory, my strength, my pain, my resurrection.

I did not read Job and say to myself, I can do it if he could do it. No, I put on Job's spirit, power and restoration. I felt him and internalized the spirit of the message. I did not see Peter as someone who was going through a similar circumstance of confusion or someone at a place of dilemma, a place of choice. I saw myself and before me was placed a choice. I saw that if I did A, then B, then C would be my harvest.

If I planted the seed offered to me through the Word I would receive the same, if not more. I felt and lived through the spirit of those I read about, I saw it, felt it, believed it, experienced it and it brought forth the truth in my life. It showed me how to overcome the lie. I wanted you to see that God asked me the same questions he asked Peter, Eve, Job, and Elijah and know that my answer is the same as theirs.

From His word he gave me the answers to the questions I had. He gave me direction and He gave me purpose. If I will believe Him and arise, I then receive the same victory.

If you don't know why you are here, I will tell you. You are here for everyone else. You are here for the fulfillment of your purpose. Purpose varies. Each person's purpose from God is unique. He whispered it to you before you entered your mother's womb. In relationship with Him all things true that are held in your spirit will be brought back into your remembrance and you will find your passion and it will lead you into purpose and ultimate fulfillment. Let the Word be your foundation on the path to revelation.

Jesus is not for us to just worship, He is our example of who we are to become. We are not poor sinners that are powerless, hoping Jesus will do all of the heavy lifting and we look pious.

He has already done the heavy lifting – the cross. Jesus cannot and will not live our lives for us. We have been given the Spirit with power to live this life and to overcome all things through Him. It is time for us to take up our cross and move in the power and Spirit of God.

We can no longer sell ourselves short or fall by the wayside as helpless and humble. God has called us to be bold and to walk in power. Put on the full armor and stand up. When Peter, Eve, Job, Elijah, Jeremiah, Gideon, Elisha, Paul and everyone else realized who they were, they walked in power, bold despite the ridicule and pressure.

I accept what God has said about me and what He told me to do despite not being a writer and always wanting to stay in the background and out of the limelight. I choose life, I choose to rise and let my light shine. My time has come and the *Glory of the Lord has Risen Upon Me!!*

I encourage you to be strong and not defeated. Please understand that sometimes you are allowed a storm, like

Job, like the disciples, like Paul, like Elijah, like Moses, like Noah, because God can trust you with the storm. He can trust you to overcome and bring forth the glory for Him that will in turn bring forth your reward and elevation. Christ has called us to say what He says and to do what He does. You need to believe in God's anointing on your life, His power. He already believes in you. You have not done anything wrong, you are here because you did everything right. Arise, shine, for your morning has come! Walk in your anointing.

Double Blessings, Zoe and Simone
(Photo by Luann List Photography)